MALTA

TRAVEL GUIDE

Essential Information and Tips to Prepare for Your Trip: Everything You Should Know Before You Go

David Günther

All rights reserved. No part of this book may be reproduced, stored in a retrieval system, or transmitted by any means, including electronic, mechanical, photocopying, recording, or otherwise, without the express written consent of the copyright holder. The content of this book is provided for general informational purposes only. The author and publisher do not guarantee the completeness, accuracy, reliability, suitability, or availability of the information, products, services, or related visuals contained in the book for any specific purpose. Any reliance on this information is solely at your own risk.

Copyright © 2024 by David Günther

TABLE OF CONTENTS

INTRODUCTION	7
CHAPTER ONE	9
GETTING ACQUAINTED WITH MALTA	9
Historical Background	*9*
Cultural Diversity	*10*
Language and Communication	*12*
Geography and Location	*14*
Climate Overview	*16*
CHAPTER TWO	19
PLANNING YOUR TRIP	19
Setting Your Malta Travel Goals	*19*
Choosing the Best Time to Visit	*21*
Visa and Entry Requirements	*24*
Health and Safety Tips	*27*
Budgeting and Money Matters	*29*
Essential Packing Checklists	*31*
Travel Friendly Luggage Options	*33*
Itinerary Suggestion: Duration of Stay	*36*
CHAPTER THREE	39
TRANSPORTATION OPTIONS	39
Getting to Malta	*39*
Getting Around in Malta	*41*
Public Transportation	41
Taxis and Ridesharing	43
Rental Cars	45
Cycling and Walking	48
Practical Transportation Tips	*51*
CHAPTER FOUR	55
ACCOMMODATION OPTIONS	55
Luxury Stays	*55*
Boutique Stays	*57*

Budget-Friendly Stays... 60
Vacation Rentals.. 63
Practical Accommodation Tips.. 65

CHAPTER FIVE... 69
Exploring Malta... 69
Top Destinations.. 69
Valletta: The Capital City.. 69
Mdina: The Silent City.. 71
Sliema and St. Julian's.. 74
The Three Cities: Vittoriosa, Senglea, and Cospicua........................ 76
Gozo Island.. 79
Comino and the Blue Lagoon... 82
Marsaxlokk and its Fishing Village Charm..................................... 85
Beaches and Swimming Spots.. 88
Popular Outdoor Activities... 91
Wellness and Spas... 95
Day Trip Options... 99

CHAPTER SIX.. 105
Entertainment And Nightlife Scene.. 105
Best Bars and Pubs in Valletta and St. Julian's................................ 105
Nightclubs and Late-Night Entertainment....................................... 108
Cultural Shows and Theatre.. 110
Live Music Venues.. 113

CHAPTER SEVEN... 117
Culinary Delights... 117
Traditional Maltese Foods: Pastizzi, Rabbit Stew, and More........ 117
Best Restaurants and Cafés... 119
Street Food and Food Market... 125
Wine and Local Spirits: Maltese Wines and Kinnie......................... 128
Where to Find the Best Seafood... 130
Foodie Travel Tips.. 133

CHAPTER EIGHT... 137
Shopping in Malta.. 137

3

    Modern Shopping Centers *137*
    Local Markets and Souvenir Shops *141*
    Specialty Shops and Boutiques *144*
    Shopping Etiquette and Tips *148*

CHAPTER NINE **151**
  CULTURAL EXPERIENCES 151
    Festivals and Events *151*
    Museums and Arts Galleries *154*
    Historical Landmarks and Heritage Sites *157*
    Religious and Spiritual Sites *161*
    Local Customs and Etiquette *164*

CHAPTER TEN **169**
  PRACTICAL INFORMATION 169
    Tourist Information Centers *169*
    Local Guides and Tour Operators *171*
    Essential Useful Phrases *174*
    Travel Insurance *176*
    Emergency Numbers and Important Contacts *179*
    Sustainable Travel Practices *181*
    Useful Apps and Websites *184*

CONCLUSION **189**
    Reflecting On Your Maltese Adventure *189*

IMPORTANT NOTE:

This travel guide is presented without images, yet it has been carefully and thoughtfully crafted to elevate your touring experience. Serving as your essential companion, the guide is designed to enrich your journey by highlighting must-visit locations, activities, and experiences. It is the result of thorough research and aims to offer a premium travel experience for all users.

While every effort has been made to ensure the accuracy of the information provided, it is advisable to complement this guide with tools like Google Maps for precise navigation and up-to-date directions to your chosen destinations. Despite the dedication to accuracy, it's important to remain mindful that changes to costs, operating hours, and other details may occur unexpectedly.

For any travel plans, bookings, or arrangements, we recommend consulting relevant authorities, companies, or online resources for the most current and reliable information. This guide is meant to be a helpful resource, offering suggestions based on the author's personal experiences and popular recommendations, rather than official endorsements.

Finally, users are encouraged to respect local laws, customs, and safety guidelines. Exercise caution and prioritize your well-being as you embark on a memorable and enjoyable travel experience.

INTRODUCTION

Welcome to Malta, a captivating archipelago nestled in the heart of the Mediterranean Sea, where the azure waters meet centuries of rich history, vibrant culture, and stunning landscapes. Known for its strategic location, Malta has long been a crossroads of civilizations, blending influences from the Phoenicians, Romans, Arabs, Normans, and the Knights of St. John. Today, it stands as one of the most unique and dynamic destinations in Europe, offering visitors an unparalleled blend of old-world charm and modern-day allure.

Malta's charm lies not only in its scenic beauty but in its deeply rooted cultural heritage. The archipelago comprises three main islands—Malta, Gozo, and Comino—each with its own distinct character. Malta, the largest and most populous island, is home to the vibrant capital city, Valletta, a UNESCO World Heritage site. With its fortified walls, historic palaces, and stunning baroque architecture, Valletta is a treasure trove of culture, art, and history. Its streets are filled with the echoes of the past, while its cafes, restaurants, and boutiques reflect the island's contemporary vibe. Just a short ferry ride away, Gozo offers a more tranquil, rural escape, famed for its lush landscapes, historic temples, and the iconic Azure Window (now sadly collapsed, but still a symbol of the island). Comino, the smallest of the three, is known for its crystal-clear waters and the famous Blue Lagoon, making it a haven for swimmers, snorkelers, and nature lovers.

The history of Malta is one of constant evolution, shaped by the various civilizations that have called it home. From the megalithic temples of Ġgantija on Gozo, some of the oldest free-standing structures in the world, to the majestic forts built by the Knights of St. John, Malta offers a journey through time. Visitors can walk in the footsteps of ancient civilizations, explore medieval citadels, or stand in awe of the baroque masterpieces that dot the islands.

The islands' Mediterranean climate is another major draw for travelers. With mild winters and warm summers, Malta is a year-round destination, offering visitors the opportunity to enjoy everything from beach holidays to cultural festivals, hiking trails, and vibrant nightlife. Whether you're exploring its historic cities, relaxing on its beaches, or indulging in its culinary delights, Malta offers a diverse and enriching experience for every traveler.

This travel guide is your trusted companion as you embark on a journey to discover Malta's many facets. We will take you through the top destinations across the islands, explore local customs, and introduce you to Malta's unique cuisine. From tips on navigating the islands' streets to insider recommendations on hidden gems, this guide will ensure you make the most of your time in Malta. Whether you are here for a weekend getaway, a cultural immersion, or an adventure in nature, we promise to help you create lasting memories. Get ready for a trip that blends the old and the new, where every corner reveals something extraordinary. Welcome to Malta—your adventure begins now!

CHAPTER ONE

GETTING ACQUAINTED WITH MALTA

Historical Background

Malta's history is a fascinating tapestry woven from the influences of numerous civilizations, each leaving its own mark on the islands. Strategically located in the heart of the Mediterranean, Malta has been a crossroads of cultures and a coveted prize for empires throughout history. Its rich historical heritage is evident in its ancient monuments, medieval fortifications, and baroque architecture, making it an essential destination for history enthusiasts.

The origins of Malta trace back to prehistoric times, with the earliest known inhabitants arriving around 5000 BCE. The megalithic temples of Ġgantija on Gozo, dating back to around 3600 BCE, are among the oldest freestanding stone structures in the world and are testament to Malta's ancient beginnings. These prehistoric communities also left behind impressive stone carvings and burial sites, which can be explored at sites like the Hypogeum of Ħal Saflieni, a subterranean complex used as a temple and burial site.

In the centuries that followed, Malta became a crossroads for several major civilizations. The Phoenicians, who established colonies on the island around 800 BCE, were among the first to influence Malta's culture and economy. The island then fell under the control of the Romans in 218 BCE, during which Malta flourished as a key part of the Roman Empire. Many of the island's Roman remains, such as villas, mosaics, and catacombs, can be explored today, with notable sites like the Roman Villa at Rabat.

After the fall of the Roman Empire, Malta was ruled by various powers, including the Byzantines, Arabs, and Normans. However, the defining chapter in Malta's history began in 1530, when the Knights of St. John, a Catholic military order, took control of the island. The Knights transformed Malta into a stronghold of Christianity and built the grand city of Valletta, a masterpiece of baroque architecture. Valletta's fortifications, grand palaces, and churches stand as a testament to their legacy and are a UNESCO World Heritage site today.

In the 19th and 20th centuries, Malta's strategic importance led it to be involved in the Napoleonic Wars and later, World War II, during which the islands played a crucial role in the Allied Mediterranean campaign. The valor shown by the Maltese people during these turbulent times earned the island the George Cross, a British decoration for courage, which is still featured on the national flag.

Today, Malta's history is reflected in its rich tapestry of landmarks and museums, including the National Museum of Archaeology in Valletta, the Inquisitor's Palace, and the impressive fortifications of the Three Cities. Visitors can walk through centuries of history, from prehistoric temples to baroque palaces, and gain a deeper appreciation for the island's role in shaping Mediterranean history.

Cultural Diversity

Malta's cultural fabric is a vibrant tapestry, woven from centuries of influences by diverse ethnicities, religions, and traditions. As a crossroads in the Mediterranean, the island has been shaped by the Phoenicians, Romans, Arabs, Normans, Knights of St. John, and more recently, the British. This long history of external influence has created a unique and harmonious blend of cultures that continues to shape the island's identity today.

The Maltese people are known for their warm hospitality and a strong sense of community. The population is predominantly Maltese, but the cultural landscape is marked by a rich mix of Mediterranean, Arab, European, and African influences. Maltese, the national language, is a Semitic language with roots in Arabic, while English is also widely spoken, reflecting Malta's colonial past. Visitors will notice the blending of these languages in everyday conversation, as well as in signage, making it easy to communicate and immerse in the local culture.

Religion plays a central role in Malta's cultural identity, with Roman Catholicism being the predominant faith. The island's religious heritage is visible in its many churches, chapels, and elaborate religious festivals. One of the most prominent cultural features is the feast day of each village's patron saint, a colorful celebration with processions, fireworks, music, and traditional feasts. These local festas are an important part of Malta's cultural calendar, creating a festive atmosphere throughout the summer months. The Feast of St. Paul's Shipwreck in Valletta and the Feast of the Assumption in Gozo are among the most significant and widely attended.

Malta's arts scene is also reflective of its diverse heritage. The islands boast a rich tradition in sculpture, painting, and architecture, especially from the baroque period, when the Knights of St. John ruled. Today, modern Maltese artists continue to create works inspired by the island's history and its Mediterranean surroundings. The National Museum of Fine Arts and the numerous galleries in Valletta showcase these artistic expressions. Music and dance also hold a special place in Maltese culture. Traditional Maltese folk music, with its distinctive rhythms and instruments like the għana (traditional singing), can be heard at festivals and local gatherings. Contemporary music, including jazz and pop, thrives in the island's dynamic nightlife.

The cuisine of Malta is another reflection of the island's cultural diversity, influenced by Italian, North African, and British flavors. Maltese dishes like pastizzi (flaky pastries filled with ricotta or peas), bragioli (beef olives), and lampuki (fish) offer a delicious fusion of local ingredients and culinary traditions. These are often enjoyed in local eateries or during family gatherings, which are an important part of the Maltese social fabric.

When visiting Malta, it's important to be mindful of local customs. The Maltese are known for their strong family values, and respect for elders is important. Dress codes are generally casual, but more formal attire is expected when visiting religious sites. Additionally, public displays of affection are reserved for more private settings, especially in more conservative areas.

Malta's cultural diversity is its greatest asset, offering travelers a unique opportunity to experience a blend of Mediterranean traditions, history, and contemporary culture. From the bustling festas to the fusion of flavors, Malta is a place where every corner offers a new cultural discovery.

Language and Communication

Malta's linguistic landscape is one of its most distinctive features, reflecting the island's diverse history and cultural influences. The official languages of Malta are Maltese and English, both of which are widely spoken throughout the islands. This dual-language heritage makes it exceptionally easy for travelers to communicate, as English is the second language for most of the population and is commonly used in business, government, and education.

Maltese: The National Language Maltese (Maltija) is the national language and is a unique blend of Semitic Arabic roots, with significant influences from Italian, English, and other European languages. It is the only official Semitic language written in the Latin alphabet, and while it may seem unfamiliar to many, the structure of the language is relatively straightforward for English speakers to pick up. While the majority of Maltese people speak Maltese fluently, the language is mostly used in daily life, family settings, and local media. Visitors will notice Maltese words and phrases in street signs, advertisements, and official documents, giving the islands a distinctive local flavor.

English: Widely Spoken As a result of Malta's history as a British colony, English has been an official language since 1814. Today, English is spoken by nearly every Maltese person and is often used in the workplace, in the media, and at tourist attractions. For travelers, this makes Malta an incredibly accessible destination, as communication is rarely a barrier. English is especially prevalent in the capital city, Valletta, and in popular tourist areas like Sliema, St. Julian's, and Gozo, where the majority of restaurants, hotels, and shops use English on signs and menus.

Communication and Etiquette While English will be sufficient for most travelers, making an effort to use a few basic phrases in Maltese can go a long way in building rapport with the locals. Simple greetings such as "Bongu" (Good morning) and "Grazzi" (Thank you) are appreciated and reflect respect for the local culture.

In terms of communication style, the Maltese are known for their warmth and friendliness. Direct communication is common, but there is a strong emphasis on politeness, especially in social settings. When addressing people, particularly elders, it's customary to show respect with appropriate greetings, such as "Sahha" (Hello) or "Bongu"

(Good morning). In more formal settings, such as when visiting churches or religious sites, it's important to be mindful of appropriate behavior, such as dressing modestly and avoiding loud conversations.

Public conversations can often be lively and expressive, with hand gestures and lively discussions being a normal part of interaction. However, it's wise to avoid controversial topics, particularly around politics or religion, unless you are familiar with the cultural context.

Non-Verbal Communication Body language in Malta can be quite expressive, and the use of hand gestures is a common way of conveying meaning in everyday conversations. This can range from a simple nod to more animated gestures. However, like in many Mediterranean cultures, excessive public displays of affection may be considered inappropriate, especially in more rural or conservative areas.

In sum, Malta is a destination where communication is made easy by the widespread use of English, but where embracing the local Maltese language and cultural nuances will enrich your experience. Whether you're asking for directions, ordering a meal, or joining in a lively conversation, understanding the local language and etiquette ensures a deeper connection with this welcoming, diverse island.

Geography and Location

Situated in the heart of the Mediterranean Sea, Malta is a small archipelago composed of three main islands—Malta, Gozo, and Comino—along with several smaller islets. Despite its modest size, Malta's geographical location has made it one of the most strategically important spots in the Mediterranean for thousands of years. Its proximity to major Mediterranean routes, just south of Italy, north of Africa, and east of Tunisia, has led to its historical significance and diverse cultural influences.

Location and Islands: The Republic of Malta is located approximately 93 kilometers (58 miles) south of Sicily, Italy, and 288 kilometers (179 miles) north of Libya, giving it a pivotal position between Europe and North Africa. The largest and most populous island, Malta, is the hub of the country's cultural, political, and economic activities. It is home to the capital city of Valletta and the majority of the country's population.

Gozo, the second-largest island, is located just a few kilometers to the northwest of Malta. Known for its tranquil atmosphere, scenic landscapes, and historic sites, Gozo offers a more rural and relaxed escape compared to the hustle and bustle of Malta's main island. Comino, the smallest of the three, lies between Malta and Gozo, famed for its crystal-clear waters and the famous Blue Lagoon, which makes it a popular spot for day-trippers and nature lovers.

In addition to the three main islands, Malta also encompasses a number of smaller islands and rocky outcrops, including Filfla and the St. Paul's Islands, which are largely uninhabited but of interest to those exploring Malta's coastal beauty.

Geography and Landscape: Malta's landscape is characterized by rugged cliffs, rocky shorelines, and sandy beaches, offering a variety of natural scenery in a relatively small area. The islands' coastlines are dotted with coves, inlets, and harbors, making it a haven for boating and water sports. The country's highest point, Ta' Dmejrek, on the island of Malta, rises just 253 meters (830 feet) above sea level, providing sweeping views of the surrounding islands.

The islands boast a Mediterranean climate, with warm summers and mild, wet winters. This climate supports a variety of flora, including Mediterranean shrubs, olive trees, and wildflowers. Although Malta lacks large forested areas, the landscape is marked by terraced fields and limestone formations that have been shaped over centuries by both natural forces and human activity. The rich biodiversity of the islands, particularly in the waters surrounding them, makes Malta an attractive destination for diving and marine exploration.

Coastal Features and Natural Attractions: Malta's coastline is one of its most captivating features. From the dramatic cliffs of Dingli and the serene beaches of Mellieħa Bay to the enchanting Blue Grotto and the secluded coves of Comino, the island offers an array of natural wonders for visitors. The Blue Lagoon on Comino is particularly famous for its crystal-clear turquoise waters, making it a perfect spot for swimming, snorkeling, and sunbathing.

Malta also boasts a number of caves and grottoes, many of which are accessible by boat, like the Blue Grotto and the caves of the coastal cliffs around Gozo. The islands' unique geological formations and rich marine life offer a distinctive environment for nature lovers.

Malta's geographic location, varied landscapes, and Mediterranean climate make it an attractive destination for travelers seeking a mix of cultural heritage and natural beauty. Whether exploring the historic cities of Valletta and Mdina or relaxing along the island's beautiful coastlines, Malta's geography enhances its appeal as a vibrant, diverse, and enchanting destination.

Climate Overview

Malta enjoys a Mediterranean climate, characterized by hot, dry summers and mild, wet winters. This pleasant weather, with over 300 sunny days each year, makes Malta a year-round destination for travelers seeking a mix of outdoor activities, cultural exploration, and coastal relaxation.

Summer (June to September): Summer in Malta is hot and dry, with temperatures often reaching 30°C (86°F) or higher, particularly in July and August. The heat can be intense, especially during midday, but the coastal breeze helps to keep things comfortable along the shoreline. The summer months also bring long, sunny days, with the sun setting late in the evening, offering plenty of daylight for outdoor activities such as sightseeing, beach visits, and water sports. This is also the peak tourist season, so popular attractions and beaches can be crowded. Travelers should dress in light, breathable clothing, use sunscreen, and stay hydrated during these months.

Autumn (October to November): Autumn is one of the most pleasant times to visit Malta, as the weather remains warm but more temperate. Daytime temperatures typically range from 20°C (68°F) to 25°C (77°F) in October and drop slightly in November. The evenings begin to cool, but it's still comfortable for outdoor dining, hiking, and exploring the island's historical sites. The sea remains warm enough for swimming into late October, and the tourist crowds thin out, making this a great time for a quieter, more relaxed experience.

Winter (December to February): Winter in Malta is mild, with temperatures ranging from 10°C (50°F) to 15°C (59°F) during the day. While the nights can get chilly, freezing temperatures are rare, and snow is virtually unheard of. Rainfall increases during the winter months, particularly in December and January, though Malta remains relatively dry compared to many other European countries. The winter season is also quieter in terms of tourism, offering a more peaceful and authentic Maltese experience. It's a great time for exploring the cultural and historical sites without the crowds, although a light jacket and umbrella may be necessary.

Spring (March to May): Spring is another wonderful time to visit Malta. Temperatures gradually warm up, reaching between 15°C (59°F) and 20°C (68°F) by May, and the island's flora comes to life with wildflowers blooming across the countryside. The weather is ideal for outdoor activities like hiking, cycling, and sightseeing, as the days are pleasant and not too hot. Rain is less frequent than in winter, and the landscape remains lush and green, making it an excellent time for nature enthusiasts and photographers to visit.

Overall Climate Considerations: Malta's climate is marked by its long, dry summer season and relatively short, mild winter. The islands' coastal position means that the sea has a moderating effect on temperatures, keeping them relatively mild throughout the year. For those who enjoy warm weather, Malta offers plenty of sunshine, while the cooler months are perfect for exploring its cultural landmarks and enjoying a more tranquil atmosphere.

Whether you're seeking a sunny beach vacation or a cultural getaway, Malta's Mediterranean climate ensures that there's something to offer at every time of year.

CHAPTER TWO

Planning Your Trip

Setting Your Malta Travel Goals

When planning a trip to Malta, one of the most important steps is setting clear travel goals. Whether you're seeking relaxation, adventure, cultural immersion, or personal growth, defining your priorities will help you create a more fulfilling and meaningful experience. Understanding what you want to achieve during your journey will guide your decisions, from choosing the right activities to crafting a personalized itinerary. Here's how to identify your travel goals and make the most of your Malta adventure.

Identify Your Travel Priorities The first step in setting your travel goals is to reflect on what you hope to achieve in Malta. Are you looking to unwind and recharge, or do you want to explore historical landmarks and immerse yourself in the local culture? Perhaps you're an adventure seeker eager to discover the island's natural beauty, or you're interested in gaining new insights through personal growth experiences.

To pinpoint your goals, consider the following categories:

- Relaxation: If you're looking for rest and rejuvenation, Malta's serene beaches, coastal walks, and wellness offerings may be your top priority.
- Exploration: If historical exploration excites you, Malta offers a wealth of ancient sites, from the megalithic temples to the baroque streets of Valletta and Mdina.

- Cultural Immersion: For those drawn to Malta's vibrant traditions, immersing yourself in local festivals, culinary experiences, and interacting with the locals may be your focus.
- Adventure: Malta's dramatic cliffs, clear waters, and opportunities for activities like hiking, scuba diving, and boat tours are ideal for the adventurous traveler.
- Personal Growth: If you're seeking self-reflection, Malta's tranquil landscapes, meditation retreats, and cultural experiences can offer the space for personal development.

Set Realistic and Achievable Goals Once you've identified your primary goals, ensure they are realistic given your time, budget, and energy levels. Malta may be a small island, but its offerings are vast, and it's easy to feel overwhelmed by all the things you want to do. Instead of cramming too many activities into your itinerary, focus on a few key goals and prioritize experiences that align with your interests. For example, if you're passionate about history, allocate more time to visiting museums and ancient ruins, and less to nightlife or shopping.

Crafting Your Itinerary A well-planned itinerary ensures that you can pursue your goals while leaving room for spontaneity. Once you've defined your objectives, create a flexible itinerary that includes your must-see sights or activities, but also allows for unstructured time. This balance will keep you from feeling rushed while still offering opportunities for exploration and enjoyment. For example, if cultural immersion is a priority, plan visits to local villages during traditional festivals or set aside time to try Malta's unique cuisine.

Maximizing Your Enjoyment To maximize your satisfaction, embrace the mindset of mindful travel. Pay attention to how each experience contributes to your overall goals. Whether it's pausing to enjoy a sunset by the sea after a day of sightseeing or taking time to chat with locals, moments of reflection can deepen your connection to Malta. Also, remain open to adjusting your plans if something unexpected arises—sometimes, the most meaningful experiences are the ones that weren't on your original list.

Setting clear travel goals for your trip to Malta will not only make your journey more enjoyable but also more meaningful. By identifying your priorities, setting realistic expectations, and creating an itinerary that aligns with your aspirations, you'll have a purposeful and rewarding experience on the islands. Let your personal goals guide your exploration of Malta, and you'll leave with memories that resonate long after you've returned home.

Choosing the Best Time to Visit

Malta's Mediterranean climate, with its warm summers and mild winters, makes it an attractive year-round destination. However, the ideal time to visit depends on your preferences for weather, activities, and overall travel experience. Here's an analysis of each season to help you decide the best time to visit Malta based on your interests and priorities.

Spring (March to May)

Spring is one of the most pleasant times to visit Malta. With daytime temperatures ranging from 15°C (59°F) to 20°C (68°F), the weather is mild and perfect for outdoor activities like sightseeing, hiking, and exploring the island's historical landmarks. Spring also offers beautiful natural scenery, as Malta's countryside is lush and green with blooming wildflowers.

This season is ideal for those who want to experience Malta without the intense summer heat or large tourist crowds. Additionally, spring is a great time to experience local festivals like the Malta International

Fireworks Festival in April or the Feast of St. Joseph in March. These events provide a wonderful cultural immersion experience.

- Advantages: Mild temperatures, fewer crowds, lush landscapes, cultural festivals
- Considerations: Sea temperatures may still be too cool for swimming in March or April
- Best for: Sightseeing, cultural festivals, outdoor exploration, nature lovers

Summer (June to August)

Summer is the peak tourist season in Malta, with long, sunny days and temperatures soaring to 30°C (86°F) or higher. The island's beautiful beaches and crystal-clear waters attract sun-seekers and water sports enthusiasts from around the world. Summer is the best time for swimming, diving, and enjoying Malta's vibrant coastal life.

While the warm weather is perfect for beach activities, summer also brings higher prices, crowded attractions, and busy beaches. If you're planning to visit during this time, be prepared for larger crowds, especially in popular areas like Valletta, the Blue Lagoon, and Gozo. Accommodation prices also tend to spike, so booking in advance is recommended.

- Advantages: Perfect beach weather, water activities, festivals, extended daylight hours
- Considerations: High temperatures, crowded attractions, higher accommodation costs
- Best for: Beach lovers, water sports enthusiasts, those seeking lively festivals

Autumn (September to November)

Autumn is a fantastic time to visit Malta, especially in September and October when the weather remains warm but more comfortable, with temperatures ranging from 20°C (68°F) to 25°C (77°F). The sea is still warm enough for swimming, and the tourist crowds begin to thin out after the summer rush.

Autumn is also harvest season, making it an excellent time to enjoy local food festivals, such as the Gozo Harvest Festival in September. With fewer tourists, you can enjoy the island's attractions at a more relaxed pace, and the cooler temperatures make it ideal for exploring historical sites and hiking.

- Advantages: Warm weather, fewer crowds, lower prices, food festivals
- Considerations: Shorter days compared to summer
- Best for: Outdoor exploration, cultural festivals, beach time without the crowds

Winter (December to February)

Winter in Malta is mild compared to most European destinations, with temperatures ranging from 10°C (50°F) to 15°C (59°F). While the weather is too cool for swimming, winter is the best time to explore the island's cultural and historical sites without the large summer crowds. Malta's UNESCO World Heritage sites, museums, and churches can be enjoyed in peace during this season.

Winter is also the time for Malta's festive season, with Christmas markets, local celebrations, and a serene atmosphere perfect for those looking for a quiet and reflective experience. Accommodation prices are lower in winter, and there are fewer tourists, making it an affordable time to visit.

- Advantages: Mild weather, fewer tourists, lower prices, festive atmosphere
- Considerations: Short days, cool temperatures, no swimming
- Best for: Cultural exploration, budget travelers, those seeking a peaceful experience

Summary of Best Times to Visit

- Best for Sightseeing and Cultural Events: Spring and autumn offer mild temperatures, fewer crowds, and a chance to experience local festivals and culture.
- Best for Beaches and Water Activities: Summer provides the warmest weather and optimal conditions for swimming, diving, and beach activities, though it comes with higher crowds and costs.
- Best for Budget Travel: Winter offers lower accommodation rates and fewer tourists, making it an affordable choice for those looking to explore Malta's cultural treasures in peace.

When choosing the best time to visit Malta, consider your interests, budget, and preferred activities. Each season offers unique advantages, ensuring that you can find the perfect time for your Malta adventure.

Visa and Entry Requirements

Before traveling to Malta, it's important to understand the visa and entry requirements to ensure a smooth arrival and avoid any surprises. Malta is a member of the European Union (EU) and the Schengen Area, which influences its visa policies. Here's an essential guide to help you navigate the entry process.

Visa-Free Travel

Citizens of the European Union (EU) and European Economic Area (EEA) countries, as well as Switzerland, do not require a visa to enter Malta. They can enter with just a valid passport or national ID card.

Additionally, citizens from several countries outside the EU, including the United States, Canada, Australia, New Zealand, Japan, and most Latin American countries, can enter Malta for short stays of up to 90 days without a visa, provided their purpose of visit is tourism, business, or family visits. Travelers from these countries can freely travel within the Schengen Area without additional documentation, but they must have a valid passport with at least three months of validity beyond the planned departure date.

Visa Requirements for Non-Visa-Exempt Countries

If you are traveling from a country that does not have a visa exemption agreement with Malta, you will need to apply for a visa before arrival. The most common visa type for short stays is the Schengen Visa, which allows travel to Malta and other Schengen Area countries.

Application Process:

- Documents: You'll need to submit a valid passport, passport-sized photos, proof of travel insurance, flight and accommodation bookings, financial statements to prove sufficient funds for your stay, and a cover letter outlining the purpose of your visit.
- Application Submission: Applications must be submitted at the nearest Maltese consulate or through an authorized visa center.

- Processing Time: Processing typically takes around 15 calendar days, but it's recommended to apply at least 3 weeks before your planned departure to account for any delays.

Visa-on-Arrival

Malta does not offer a visa-on-arrival option for most travelers. Therefore, it's essential to obtain the necessary visa before your trip if required.

Special Permits and Documentation

For specific activities or regions within Malta, additional permits may be required:

- Work Permits: If you plan to work in Malta, you will need a work permit, and this typically requires securing a job offer first.
- Student Visas: Those wishing to study in Malta for longer than 90 days must apply for a student visa.
- Schengen Zone Travel: If your visa is for Malta and you intend to travel to other Schengen countries, ensure that you meet the Schengen visa requirements for entry and stay.

Tips for a Smooth Arrival

- Ensure your passport is valid for at least three months beyond your planned departure date from Malta.
- Always double-check visa requirements based on your nationality, as they may vary.
- Be prepared to show proof of funds and a return ticket to demonstrate that you will leave the country at the end of your permitted stay.

By understanding and preparing for Malta's visa and entry requirements, you can ensure a seamless and hassle-free arrival for your trip.

Health and Safety Tips

When visiting Malta, maintaining good health and ensuring your safety are key to enjoying a worry-free trip. As a safe and traveler-friendly destination, Malta offers reliable healthcare and a low crime rate, but it's still important to be prepared. Here's a guide to staying healthy and safe during your visit.

Health Tips

1. Vaccinations

No special vaccinations are required for entry to Malta. However, it's a good idea to ensure routine vaccines like measles, mumps, rubella (MMR), diphtheria, tetanus, and influenza are up to date.

2. Healthcare System

Malta boasts a high standard of healthcare, with both public and private hospitals providing excellent services. EU nationals can use their European Health Insurance Card (EHIC) to access public healthcare at reduced costs. Non-EU travelers are advised to purchase comprehensive travel insurance that covers medical emergencies.

3. Food and Water Safety

Tap water in Malta is generally safe to drink, but it's desalinated and may have a distinct taste. Bottled water is widely available and often preferred by visitors. Enjoy Malta's cuisine at restaurants and street markets, but ensure food is cooked thoroughly, especially seafood.

4. Sun Protection

Malta's Mediterranean climate means plenty of sunshine, even in winter. Protect yourself from sunburn by using sunscreen, wearing a hat and sunglasses, and staying hydrated, particularly during the summer months.

5. Emergency Numbers

For emergencies, dial 112 for ambulance, police, or fire services. Pharmacies are readily available and can provide over-the-counter medications for minor ailments.

Safety Tips

1. Low Crime Rate

Malta is considered a safe destination with a very low crime rate. However, like anywhere, pickpocketing can occur in crowded tourist areas. Keep valuables secure, and avoid leaving belongings unattended.

2. Swimming and Water Safety

Malta's beaches and coastal areas are stunning, but pay attention to safety signs and flags at swimming spots. Avoid swimming in rough seas or at unmarked locations. Be cautious when exploring rocky areas, as they can be slippery.

3. Road Safety

Driving in Malta is on the left side of the road. Roads can be narrow, and local drivers may be assertive. If renting a car, drive cautiously, especially in urban areas. For pedestrians, exercise caution when crossing streets, as traffic can be busy in towns and cities.

4. Adventure Activities

Malta offers activities like scuba diving, hiking, and sailing. Use licensed operators for these activities to ensure safety standards are met. Always follow guides' instructions and wear appropriate gear.

5. Local Laws and Customs

Respect Maltese laws and customs, such as dress codes when visiting religious sites. Avoid littering, as the Maltese value their environment, and heavy fines can apply.

By following these health and safety tips, you can fully enjoy Malta's rich history, stunning landscapes, and vibrant culture with peace of mind.

Budgeting and Money Matters

Planning your finances is a crucial step to ensuring a stress-free and enjoyable trip to Malta. This guide provides practical advice to help you manage your money, save costs, and handle finances securely while exploring this beautiful Mediterranean destination.

Currency and Payment Methods

Malta uses the Euro (€). Currency exchange options include banks, exchange offices, and ATMs, which are widely available across the islands. ATMs usually offer the best exchange rates but may charge withdrawal fees, so check with your bank beforehand. Most businesses in Malta accept credit and debit cards, but it's wise to carry some cash for smaller establishments or local markets, especially in rural areas.

Tips:

- Use exchange offices with no commission fees, typically found in tourist areas or airports.
- Notify your bank of your travel dates to avoid any card blocks.
- Avoid dynamic currency conversion at ATMs or card terminals, which often results in unfavorable exchange rates.

Creating a Travel Budget

Estimate your expenses for a well-planned trip:

- Accommodation: Options range from budget hostels (€15–€30/night) to mid-range hotels (€60–€120/night) and luxury stays (€150+).
- Meals: Dining at local eateries may cost €10–€20 per meal, while upscale restaurants can range from €30–€50 per person.
- Transportation: Public buses cost €1.50–€2 per ride, and weekly bus passes are available for €21. Taxis and car rentals cost more (€40/day for rentals).
- Activities: Entry to museums or attractions costs €5–€15, while scuba diving or boat tours can range from €40–€80.
- Souvenirs: Budget €20–€50 for local crafts or keepsakes.
- Emergencies: Set aside a contingency fund for unexpected expenses like medical needs or delayed travel.

Money-Saving Strategies

- Use public transportation instead of taxis or rental cars for affordable travel.
- Stay at guesthouses or Airbnb rentals to save on accommodation.
- Dine at local eateries, such as traditional bakeries or casual trattorias, rather than touristy restaurants.

- Seek out free attractions, like exploring Malta's ancient streets, hiking trails, or public beaches.
- Look for discounts on attractions or group passes for museums and heritage sites.

Managing Finances Securely

- Keep cash and valuables in a money belt or hotel safe.
- Split your payment methods—carry some cash, a primary card, and a backup card in separate locations.
- Monitor your bank and credit card transactions for any unauthorized charges.
- Avoid using public Wi-Fi for online banking or financial transactions.

With smart planning, careful budgeting, and secure money management, you can enjoy Malta's rich culture, history, and beauty while staying financially stress-free.

Essential Packing Checklists

Packing smartly for your trip to Malta ensures you're well-prepared to enjoy its sunny weather, cultural landmarks, and seaside adventures. This guide provides tailored checklists for different travelers, plus tips for packing efficiently and meeting Malta's unique needs.

General Packing Essentials

- Travel Documents:
    - Passport (with at least six months validity)
    - Visa (if required)
    - Travel insurance details
    - Flight and accommodation confirmations
    - Emergency contact information

- Clothing:
  - Lightweight, breathable clothes for the warm Mediterranean climate (t-shirts, shorts, sundresses)
  - Swimwear and a cover-up for beaches or pools
  - A light sweater or jacket for cooler evenings (especially in spring and winter)
  - Comfortable walking shoes for exploring historical sites and city streets
  - Sandals for the beach
- Toiletries:
  - Sunscreen (high SPF)
  - After-sun lotion
  - Insect repellent
  - Travel-sized shampoo, soap, and toothpaste
  - Medications (prescription and over-the-counter essentials)
- Electronics:
  - Power adapter (Malta uses Type G sockets)
  - Portable charger for phones and devices
  - Camera or smartphone for photos
  - Waterproof phone pouch for beach or water activities
- Accessories:
  - Hat and sunglasses for sun protection
  - Reusable water bottle (hydration is crucial)
  - Daypack for daily excursions
  - Beach towel

Special Considerations for Activities

- Beach Lovers:
  - Snorkeling gear (if preferred)
  - Waterproof sandals or water shoes for rocky beaches

- - Quick-dry towel
- Cultural Explorers:
  - Modest attire for visiting churches or religious sites (scarves or shawls for covering shoulders)
  - Guidebooks or maps
  - Notebook for jotting down observations
- Adventure Seekers:
  - Sturdy hiking shoes for trails in Gozo or Dingli Cliffs
  - Lightweight rain jacket for unpredictable weather
  - Compact first-aid kit

Efficient Packing Tips

- Pack Light: Use a carry-on suitcase or backpack to minimize hassle. Roll clothes to save space.
- Layering is Key: For Malta's variable shoulder-season weather, layering ensures comfort.
- Plan Ahead: Match outfits to your itinerary and avoid overpacking.
- Leave Room for Souvenirs: Malta is known for unique crafts like lace and ceramics, so leave space for mementos.

With this checklist, you'll be ready for Malta's sunny beaches, historic sites, and vibrant culture without forgetting anything important!

Travel Friendly Luggage Options

Choosing the right luggage is essential for a comfortable and hassle-free trip to Malta. The destination's diverse experiences, from historical sightseeing to beach relaxation, call for smart luggage decisions. Here's a guide to selecting travel-friendly luggage and packing efficiently.

Types of Luggage

- Suitcases:
  - Advantages: Hard-shell suitcases offer excellent protection for fragile items, while soft-sided ones are more flexible for packing extra items.
  - Limitations: Less convenient on uneven surfaces, such as cobblestone streets in Valletta.
- Backpacks:
  - Advantages: Ideal for light travelers or adventurers exploring multiple islands. Comfortable and hands-free.
  - Limitations: Limited space and organization. Can strain your back if overpacked.
- Duffel Bags:
  - Advantages: Lightweight and flexible, making them suitable for short trips or beach vacations.
  - Limitations: Lack of structure and can be tiring to carry for long distances.
- Carry-On Bags:
  - Advantages: Perfect for short stays or minimalists. Avoids checked luggage fees.
  - Limitations: Limited space for extended trips or souvenirs.

Factors to Consider

- Size and Weight: Choose luggage that complies with airline regulations. Lightweight options maximize packing space within weight limits.
- Durability: Hard-shell materials like polycarbonate are durable, while high-denier nylon suits soft-sided bags.

- Security Features: Look for TSA-approved locks, tamper-resistant zippers, and RFID-blocking compartments for added security.
- Handling Ease: Opt for luggage with smooth, multi-directional wheels and a sturdy telescoping handle for maneuvering in busy streets or airports.

Packing Techniques

- Use Packing Cubes: These organize items by category, making it easy to find things and repack efficiently.
- Compression Bags: Compress bulky clothing like jackets to save space.
- Roll Clothes: Rolling reduces wrinkles and maximizes space.
- Limit Liquids: Use travel-sized bottles and comply with airline restrictions to avoid spills or delays.
- Layer Strategically: Place heavier items at the bottom for suitcases and closer to your back in backpacks.

Travel Accessories

- Luggage Locks: Keep your belongings secure. TSA-approved locks are ideal for checked luggage.
- Luggage Trackers: Devices like AirTags help locate lost luggage quickly.
- Portable Luggage Scale: Avoid overweight baggage fees by weighing bags before heading to the airport.
- Waterproof Covers: Protect bags from unexpected rain or splashes during ferry rides.

By selecting luggage suited to your needs and following these packing tips, you'll ensure a smooth, organized, and enjoyable trip to Malta!

Itinerary Suggestion: Duration of Stay

Malta's compact size and diverse attractions make it an ideal destination for travelers of all interests. Whether you're visiting for a weekend getaway, a week-long holiday, or an extended stay, you can tailor your itinerary to suit your travel style. Here are suggested itineraries for different durations and types of travelers.

Weekend Getaway (2–3 Days)

- Perfect for: Time-strapped travelers seeking a quick taste of Malta.
    - Day 1: Arrive in Valletta and explore the capital's highlights, including St. John's Co-Cathedral, the Grandmaster's Palace, and Upper Barrakka Gardens. End the day with a harbor cruise for stunning views of the city's fortifications.
    - Day 2: Visit the ancient city of Mdina, known as the Silent City. Explore its narrow streets, panoramic views, and historical sites. In the afternoon, head to the Blue Grotto for a boat tour and admire the natural sea caves.
    - Day 3: Spend the morning at one of Malta's sandy beaches, such as Mellieħa Bay. If time allows, visit Marsaxlokk, a traditional fishing village known for its colorful boats and Sunday market.

Week-Long Holiday (6–7 Days)

- Perfect for: Travelers who want to explore Malta's history, nature, and culture at a relaxed pace.
    - Day 1–2: Follow the weekend itinerary to cover Valletta and Mdina.
    - Day 3: Take a ferry to Gozo. Visit the Ġgantija Temples, a UNESCO World Heritage site, and enjoy the picturesque

town of Victoria. Explore the Azure Window ruins at Dwejra and unwind at Ramla Bay.
- Day 4: Spend a full day at the island of Comino. Snorkel in the Blue Lagoon's turquoise waters and hike its trails for breathtaking views.
- Day 5: Dive into Malta's maritime heritage with a visit to the Malta Maritime Museum and Fort St. Angelo in Birgu. Enjoy dinner along the scenic Birgu Waterfront.
- Day 6: Tour the Three Cities (Birgu, Senglea, and Cospicua) to discover their historic charm. In the afternoon, visit the prehistoric Ħaġar Qim and Mnajdra Temples.
- Day 7: Relax at Golden Bay beach or enjoy watersports. Wrap up with a traditional Maltese feast at a local restaurant.

Extended Stay (10+ Days)

- Perfect for: Slow travelers, families, and adventure seekers who want to experience Malta in depth.
  - Days 1–7: Follow the week-long itinerary for a thorough exploration.
  - Day 8–9: Dive deeper into Malta's countryside with hiking or cycling trails in Gozo or Dingli Cliffs. Visit smaller villages like Żebbuġ or Għar Lapsi to experience authentic Maltese life.
  - Day 10: Explore Malta's vibrant arts and cultural scene, including museums, galleries, and theaters like the Manoel Theatre. Attend a local festival if your trip coincides with one.

- Additional Days: Learn diving or sailing, join a food and wine tour, or take a cooking class to master Maltese cuisine.

Tips for Different Types of Travelers

- History Buffs: Prioritize Valletta, Mdina, and the prehistoric temples. Add the Hypogeum of Ħal Saflieni for a unique archaeological experience.
- Beach Lovers: Dedicate more time to Comino, Mellieħa Bay, Golden Bay, and St. Peter's Pool.
- Adventurers: Include scuba diving at famous sites like the Blue Hole or HMS Maori wreck, and hiking trails in Gozo.
- Families: Explore family-friendly attractions like Popeye Village, Malta National Aquarium, and safe beaches with shallow waters.

Whether you're seeking relaxation, adventure, or cultural immersion, Malta offers something for everyone. Plan your itinerary wisely to make the most of your stay in this Mediterranean gem.

CHAPTER THREE

TRANSPORTATION OPTIONS

Getting to Malta

Malta, an island nation in the Mediterranean Sea, is easily accessible via international flights, ferries, and cruises. With efficient travel options, planning your journey to this captivating destination is simple. Here's a comprehensive guide to reaching Malta and connecting to key locations upon arrival.

International Flights

Malta International Airport (MLA) in Luqa is the island's sole airport and a primary gateway for visitors. It hosts a range of international flights, including major carriers and budget airlines, from cities across Europe, North Africa, and the Middle East.

- Direct Flights: Direct connections are available from major hubs like London, Rome, Paris, Frankfurt, Istanbul, and Dubai. Budget airlines such as Ryanair and easyJet offer affordable options from Europe.
- Travel Time: Flights from most European cities average 2–3 hours.
- Costs: Prices vary by season, with lower fares often available during Malta's off-peak months (November–March).
- Booking Tips: Book flights early, especially during the summer high season, to secure better deals. Flexible dates can help reduce costs.

Upon arrival at MLA, taxis, ride-hailing services, and airport shuttles provide easy transportation to key destinations, including Valletta (15 minutes), Sliema (20 minutes), and St. Julian's (25 minutes). Public buses also operate from the airport and are an economical option.

Ferries to Malta

Ferries are a popular choice for travelers from nearby Sicily or for those on a Mediterranean road trip.

- Sicily-Malta Routes: High-speed ferries operated by Virtu Ferries run between Pozzallo or Catania (Sicily) and Valletta.
    o Travel Time: 1.5–4 hours, depending on the route.
    o Costs: Approximately €60–€120 per passenger (round-trip), with additional fees for vehicles.
- Booking Tips: Advance booking is recommended during summer months. Check weather conditions as rough seas may impact schedules.

The ferry terminal in Valletta is close to the city center, with taxis and buses available for onward travel.

Cruises to Malta

As a popular stop on Mediterranean cruise itineraries, Malta welcomes numerous luxury liners at the Valletta Cruise Port, situated in the historic Grand Harbour.

- Travelers on Cruises: Typically spend a day exploring Valletta, the Three Cities, or nearby attractions before returning to the ship.
- Independent Travel: Disembarking passengers can easily access taxis, ride-hailing services, or guided tours to maximize their visit.

Connecting Transportation Within Malta

- Public Buses: Malta has an extensive bus network connecting Valletta, major towns, beaches, and attractions. The Tallinja Card offers discounts for frequent users.
- Car Rentals: Ideal for travelers exploring remote areas or visiting Gozo. Left-hand driving is standard.
- Ferries to Gozo and Comino: Gozo Channel ferries operate from Ċirkewwa to Gozo, while smaller boats run to Comino.

Whether arriving by air, sea, or cruise, Malta's well-connected transport options ensure a seamless journey to this Mediterranean paradise.

Getting Around in Malta

Public Transportation

Malta offers an efficient and affordable public transportation system, making it easy for visitors to explore the island and its diverse attractions. The network includes buses, ferries, and the ferry service to Gozo, all of which are well-connected, punctual, and accessible. Here's a detailed look at the available public transportation options in Malta, including routes, schedules, and fare information.

Public Buses

Malta's bus network, operated by Malta Public Transport, serves the entire island, including key towns, beaches, and tourist attractions. Buses are the most convenient and cost-effective way to travel within Malta.

- Routes: The bus network covers most major destinations, including Valletta, Sliema, St. Julian's, Mdina, and the airport.

Popular routes also connect to coastal areas, including Golden Bay, Mellieħa Bay, and the Blue Grotto.
- Schedules: Buses run frequently from 5:30 AM to 11:30 PM, with some routes offering extended service during the summer months. On weekends and holidays, schedules may be adjusted. You can find detailed timetables at bus stops or on the Malta Public Transport website and mobile app.
- Fares:
    - Adult single fare: €2 for a standard ticket (higher during summer months).
    - Tallinja Card: A prepaid travel card that offers discounted fares. The Adult Tallinja Card offers unlimited travel for €21 for 7 days, making it ideal for tourists.
    - Night Buses: Night bus services are available on select routes after 11:30 PM, providing an affordable travel option for late-night arrivals or departures.
- Tickets are available on buses, at vending machines, or through the mobile app, but the Tallinja Card offers the best value for frequent travelers.

Ferries and Water Transport

Malta's ferry system offers convenient travel options for both locals and tourists, especially for those visiting Gozo and Comino.

- Gozo Channel Ferries: These ferries connect the main island of Malta with the sister island of Gozo. The ferry departs from Ċirkewwa (Malta) to Mġarr (Gozo) every 45 minutes.
    - Travel Time: Approximately 25 minutes.
    - Fares:
        - Passengers: €4.65 one-way (return ticket available).

- o Vehicles: Additional charges apply for cars and motorbikes.
- Ferries run 24 hours a day, with increased service in summer months.
- Comino Ferries: Smaller boats connect Malta to Comino, particularly to the Blue Lagoon, a popular destination for snorkeling and swimming.

Ferry Services within Valletta

A popular and scenic option is the Valletta Ferry, which connects Valletta to Sliema and the Three Cities.

- Travel Time: Approximately 10 minutes.
- Fare: €2 per trip.

Practical Tips

- Mobile App: Download the Tallinja Bus app for live updates, timetables, and easy access to digital tickets.
- Accessibility: Most buses are wheelchair-accessible, and there are dedicated services for those with special needs.

Public transportation in Malta offers convenience, affordability, and wide coverage, making it an ideal choice for getting around the island.

Taxis and Ridesharing

Malta, despite its small size, offers a variety of transportation options for both locals and tourists. Taxis and ride-sharing services are readily available, providing convenient ways to navigate the islands.

Taxis:

Traditional taxis can be found at designated ranks, hailed on the street, or booked by phone. White taxis are the standard, operating on fixed rates for certain routes, especially airport transfers. It's advisable to confirm the fare with the driver before starting your journey or ensure the meter is running.

Ride-Sharing Services:

Ride-sharing has gained immense popularity in Malta, offering a more flexible and often cheaper alternative to traditional taxis. The primary players are:

- Bolt: This Estonian company is the most popular ride-hailing service in Malta, known for its competitive pricing and widespread availability.
- Uber: The global giant also operates in Malta, providing its familiar ride-hailing platform.
- eCabs: A local Maltese company, eCabs offers a strong alternative with a user-friendly app and a good reputation.

Approximate Costs:

- Airport transfer (e.g., to Sliema/St. Julian's):
    - Taxi: €20-€30
    - Ride-sharing: €15-€20
- Short trips within urban areas:
    - Taxi: €10-€15
    - Ride-sharing: €5-€10

These are rough estimates, and actual fares can vary depending on traffic, time of day, and specific routes. Ride-sharing apps typically provide fare estimates before you book a ride.

Unique Considerations and Regulations:

- Regulation: Malta has regulations in place for both taxis and ride-sharing services, ensuring safety and service standards.

- Drivers need to be licensed and vehicles must meet certain requirements.
- Availability: Both taxis and ride-sharing are generally readily available across Malta, especially in popular tourist areas. However, during peak hours or late nights, you might experience slightly longer waiting times.
- Gozo: While taxis operate on Gozo, ride-sharing services have expanded their presence there as well, offering more convenient options for exploring the sister island.
- App Usage: For ride-sharing, downloading the respective apps (Bolt, Uber, eCabs) is essential. These apps allow you to book rides, track your driver, and make cashless payments.

Overall, Malta offers a well-developed system of taxis and ride-sharing services, providing visitors with various options to get around comfortably and efficiently.

Rental Cars

Renting a car in Malta offers the freedom to explore the islands at your own pace, venturing beyond the usual tourist routes and discovering hidden gems. Here's a comprehensive guide to help you navigate the process:

Rental Agencies and Locations:

Numerous international and local car rental agencies operate in Malta, offering a wide range of vehicles to suit different needs and budgets. Some of the popular agencies include:

- International Brands: Hertz, Avis, Europcar, Sixt
- Local Companies: Drifter, Malta First Car Hire, Gold Car Rental

These agencies have offices at Malta International Airport (MLA) and in various towns and cities across the islands, including Valletta, Sliema, and St. Julian's.

Driving Regulations:

- Driving Side: Malta follows left-hand traffic, similar to the UK.
- Driving License: A valid international driving permit (IDP) is recommended for non-EU citizens, although most national driving licenses are accepted.
- Age Restrictions: The minimum driving age is 18, but most rental companies require drivers to be at least 21 and have held a license for a year or more.
- Speed Limits: Generally 50 km/h (31 mph) in urban areas and 80 km/h (50 mph) on open roads.
- Seatbelts: Mandatory for all passengers.
- Alcohol Limit: 0.08% blood alcohol content.

Considerations When Renting a Car:

- Car Size: Consider a smaller car due to narrow roads and limited parking spaces, especially in historic towns.
- Insurance: Ensure you have adequate insurance coverage, including Collision Damage Waiver (CDW) and Third Party Liability.
- Manual vs. Automatic: Manual transmissions are more common, so specify if you require an automatic.
- Booking in Advance: Booking your rental car in advance, especially during peak season, is advisable to secure better rates and availability.

Popular Road Trip Routes:

- Coastal Drive: Explore the scenic coastal roads, passing through picturesque villages, cliffs, and beaches.
- Valletta and the Three Cities: Discover the historic capital city and the fortified cities of Vittoriosa, Senglea, and Cospicua.
- Mdina and Rabat: Visit the ancient walled city of Mdina and its charming neighbor Rabat, with their historical sites and panoramic views.
- Gozo Island: Take a ferry to Gozo and explore its tranquil landscapes, charming villages, and stunning coastline.

Tips for Navigating Local Traffic and Parking:

- Traffic: Be prepared for heavy traffic, especially during peak hours in urban areas.
- Road Conditions: Some roads, particularly in rural areas, can be narrow and winding.
- Roundabouts: Malta has numerous roundabouts, so be familiar with the rules of navigating them.
- Parking: Parking can be challenging in popular areas. Look for designated parking zones or use public parking facilities.
- Local Driving Style: Be aware that some local drivers may have a more assertive driving style.

Additional Tips:

- Use a GPS or map: This will help you navigate the roads and find your way around.
- Be patient: Traffic can be unpredictable, so allow extra time for your journeys.
- Respect local regulations: Adhere to speed limits and parking restrictions.

- Enjoy the scenery: Take your time and appreciate the beautiful landscapes and charming towns.

By following these tips and being prepared, you can enjoy a safe and rewarding driving experience in Malta, exploring the islands at your own pace and discovering their hidden treasures.

Cycling and Walking

Malta, with its compact size and varied landscapes, offers opportunities for exploring on foot and by bicycle. While traffic can be a concern for cycling in some areas, there are still enjoyable routes and pedestrian areas to discover.

Pedestrian-Friendly Areas:

Valletta: The capital city, a UNESCO World Heritage site, features a grid layout and many pedestrianized streets, making it ideal for walking. Explore its historic architecture, gardens (like the Upper Barrakka Gardens), and the Valletta Waterfront.

Mdina: The "Silent City" is largely pedestrianized, offering a peaceful atmosphere for strolling through its narrow streets and enjoying panoramic views from the city walls.

Sliema Promenade: This long promenade along the coastline provides beautiful sea views and a pleasant walk or jog. It's also popular for evening strolls.

The Three Cities (Vittoriosa, Senglea, Cospicua): These historic fortified cities offer narrow, winding streets perfect for exploring on foot, discovering hidden gems, and enjoying the waterfront areas.

Gozo's Citadel (Citadella): Located in Victoria, Gozo, the Citadel is a charming pedestrianized area with historic buildings and stunning views of the island.

Popular Cycling Routes:

While traffic in Malta can be challenging for cycling in some areas, certain routes offer a more pleasant experience:

- Coastal Roads (especially in less congested areas): Some coastal roads outside the main urban centers offer scenic views and less traffic. However, be cautious of narrow roads and limited shoulders. The northern and western coasts of Malta, and much of Gozo, offer better cycling experiences.
- Gozo: Gozo is generally more suitable for cycling than Malta, with quieter roads, rolling hills, and beautiful countryside. The island's smaller size makes it easier to explore by bike. Consider routes along the coast or inland through villages.
- Designated Cycle Paths (Limited): Malta has a limited network of dedicated cycle paths. Check local resources or maps for the most up-to-date information on available routes. The promenade areas are often shared use paths.

Bike Rental Services and Shops:

- Several bike rental shops operate in Malta, offering various types of bikes, including city bikes, mountain bikes, road bikes, and e-bikes. Some options include:
- Nextbike Malta: This is a public bike-sharing scheme with docking stations in various locations. It's convenient for short trips within urban areas.
- Local Bike Shops: Many bike shops in tourist areas like Sliema, St. Julian's, Bugibba, and Mellieha offer rentals. Search online for "bike rental Malta" or ask at your accommodation for local recommendations.

Services offered often include:

- Bike rental (hourly, daily, or weekly rates)
- Helmets and locks
- Maps and route suggestions
- Bike repairs and maintenance
- Sometimes guided tours

Safety Considerations:

- Traffic: Be extremely cautious of traffic, especially in urban areas. Maltese roads can be busy and narrow, and drivers may not always be considerate of cyclists.
- Helmets: Wearing a helmet is highly recommended for all cyclists.
- Visibility: Wear bright clothing and use lights (front and rear), especially when cycling at night or in low-light conditions.
- Road Conditions: Be aware of road conditions, as some roads may have potholes or uneven surfaces.
- Weather: Malta's summers can be hot, so stay hydrated and wear sunscreen.
- Pedestrians: Be considerate of pedestrians, especially in pedestrianized areas and on shared-use paths.
- Gozo Ferry: If taking your bike to Gozo, check the ferry schedule and any specific regulations for transporting bicycles.

Walking is an excellent way to explore Malta's historic cities and coastal areas. While cycling in Malta requires extra caution due to traffic, Gozo offers a more relaxed and enjoyable cycling experience. By prioritizing safety and choosing appropriate routes, you can enjoy exploring the Maltese Islands on foot and by bike.

Practical Transportation Tips

Navigating Malta efficiently is key to maximizing your travel experience. This section provides actionable advice on using the island's various transportation options, ensuring a smooth and confident journey.

Public Transportation (Buses):

- Extensive Network: Malta Public Transport operates an extensive bus network covering most of Malta and Gozo. Buses are a cost-effective way to travel between towns and villages.
- Tallinja Card: For frequent bus users, the Tallinja Card offers significant savings. Several options are available, including:
    - ExplorePlus Meep Card: Offers unlimited travel for a set number of days, including ferry services. Ideal for tourists.
    - 12 Single Day Journeys: For those who prefer to pay as they go.
- Tallinja App: Download the Tallinja App for real-time bus tracking, route planning, journey information, and mobile ticketing. It's an essential tool for navigating the bus system.
- Cash Fares: Single journey tickets can be purchased on the bus, but having exact change is recommended.
- Peak Hours: Buses can be very crowded during peak hours (typically mornings and late afternoons/early evenings, especially on weekdays). Be prepared for potential delays.
- Night Buses: Night bus routes operate between certain locations, primarily on weekends. Check the Tallinja App for schedules.

- Accessibility: Many buses are equipped with ramps and designated spaces for wheelchairs. Check the Tallinja App or website for specific route information.

Ferry Services:

- Valletta to Three Cities: Regular ferry services connect Valletta to the Three Cities (Birgu, Senglea, and Cospicua), offering a scenic and quick way to travel across the Grand Harbour.
- Malta to Gozo: A regular ferry service operates between Ċirkewwa (Malta) and Mġarr (Gozo). The journey takes approximately 25 minutes.
- Comino Ferries: Smaller ferries and boat tours operate to Comino, primarily to the Blue Lagoon.
- Ticketing: Tickets can be purchased at ferry terminals. Consider purchasing return tickets for better value.
- Schedules: Check ferry schedules in advance, as they can vary depending on the season and weather conditions.

Taxis:

- White Taxis: Malta's official taxis are white. They can be found at taxi stands, hailed on the street, or booked by phone.
- Fixed Rates: Some routes, particularly airport transfers, have fixed rates. Always confirm the fare with the driver before starting your journey, especially for non-fixed routes, or ensure the meter is running.
- Pre-Booking: Pre-booking a taxi is recommended for airport transfers or early morning departures.

Ride-Sharing (Bolt, eCabs):

- Convenient and Often Cheaper: Ride-hailing services like Bolt and eCabs are widely available and often offer more competitive fares than traditional taxis.
- App-Based: Download the respective apps before arriving in Malta.
- Fare Estimates: The apps provide fare estimates before you book a ride.
- Payment: Payment is typically handled through the app using a linked credit or debit card.

Car and Scooter Rentals:

- Flexibility: Renting a car or scooter provides greater flexibility for exploring the islands at your own pace.
- Narrow Roads and Traffic: Be prepared for narrow roads, heavy traffic (especially in urban areas), and limited parking.
- Driving on the Left: Remember that driving is on the left-hand side of the road.
- Parking: Parking can be challenging in popular tourist areas. Look for designated parking zones or use public car parks.
- Insurance: Ensure you have adequate insurance coverage.
- Scooter Considerations: If renting a scooter, wear a helmet and be extra cautious of traffic.

Eco-Friendly Transportation:

- Walking: Walking is an excellent way to explore many areas, especially within cities and towns.
- Cycling: Consider cycling, especially on Gozo, for a more eco-friendly way to get around.
- Electric Bikes and Scooters: Some rental companies offer electric bikes and scooters.

- Public Transport: Using public transport (buses and ferries) is a more sustainable option than private vehicles.

Safety and Accessibility:

- Road Safety: Be aware of local traffic conditions and drive defensively.
- Pedestrian Safety: Use designated crosswalks and be cautious of traffic.
- Accessibility: While efforts are being made to improve accessibility, some areas, especially historic sites, may have limited accessibility for people with mobility issues. Check accessibility information in advance.

Key Takeaways for Efficient Travel:

- Plan your journeys in advance: Use the Tallinja App or Google Maps to plan your routes and check schedules.
- Consider a Tallinja Card: If you plan on using buses frequently.
- Be aware of peak travel times: Especially on buses.
- Use ride-sharing services for convenient and often cheaper travel: Compared to taxis.
- Walk whenever possible: To explore cities and towns.
- Prioritize safety: Regardless of your chosen mode of transport.

By following these practical transportation tips, you can navigate Malta with ease and confidence, making the most of your time on this beautiful island nation.

CHAPTER FOUR

Accommodation Options

Malta offers a diverse range of accommodation to suit every traveler and budget. From luxurious five-star hotels with stunning sea views and world-class amenities to charming boutique hotels nestled in historic towns, there's something for everyone. Options also include self-catering apartments and guesthouses, providing a more independent and budget-friendly experience. Whether you seek pampering or a local immersion, Malta has the perfect place to call home during your stay.

Luxury Stays

Malta, with its rich history and stunning landscapes, offers a selection of exceptional luxury accommodations that cater to discerning travelers seeking unparalleled indulgence. These prestigious hotels provide opulent features, impeccable service, and unique experiences, ensuring an unforgettable stay.

The Phoenicia Malta (Valletta):

Located just outside Valletta's city walls, The Phoenicia is an iconic landmark hotel exuding timeless elegance. Its Art Deco architecture and meticulously landscaped gardens offer a tranquil escape.

- Address: The Mall, Floriana, FRN1478, Malta
- Amenities: Outdoor infinity pool overlooking the Grand Harbour, spa with signature treatments, fitness center, multiple bars and lounges.
- Services: 24-hour concierge, personalized service, in-room dining, valet parking.

- Dining: Diverse culinary experiences, from fine dining at the Phoenix Restaurant to casual meals at the Palm Court Lounge.
- Exclusive Experiences: Private historical tours, personalized yacht charters, exclusive access to cultural events.

Iniala Harbour House (Valletta):

Nestled within Valletta's historic bastions, Iniala Harbour House offers a unique blend of contemporary design and historical charm. Each suite is individually designed by renowned international designers.

- Address: 11 St Barbara Bastion, Valletta, VLT 1961, Malta
- Amenities: Rooftop pool with panoramic harbour views, spa offering bespoke treatments, fitness centre.
- Services: Dedicated concierge service, personalized itineraries, private transfers.
- Dining: Michelin-starred ION – The Harbour restaurant offering innovative cuisine with breathtaking views.
- Exclusive Experiences: Private dining experiences with renowned chefs, curated art tours, exclusive access to historical sites.

Kempinski Hotel San Lawrenz (Gozo):

Located on the tranquil island of Gozo, the Kempinski Hotel San Lawrenz provides a serene retreat surrounded by lush countryside.

- Address: Triq ir-Rokon, San Lawrenz, Gozo, SLZ 1040, Malta
- Amenities: Multiple swimming pools, including indoor and outdoor options, a luxurious spa with Ayurvedic treatments, fitness center, tennis courts.
- Services: Dedicated concierge service, personalized excursions, private transfers.

- Dining: Several restaurants and bars offering diverse culinary experiences, from Mediterranean cuisine to international flavors.
- Exclusive Experiences: Private boat trips to Comino's Blue Lagoon, customized wellness retreats, wine tasting experiences.

These luxury hotels stand out due to:

- Prime Locations: Situated in prime locations, offering easy access to key attractions and stunning views.
- Exceptional Design: Showcasing exquisite architecture, elegant interiors, and meticulous attention to detail.
- Personalized Service: Providing dedicated concierge services, personalized itineraries, and anticipating every guest's need.
- Exclusive Experiences: Offering unique and curated experiences that go beyond the typical tourist offerings.

These luxurious stays offer discerning travelers the epitome of Maltese hospitality and indulgence, ensuring an unforgettable experience filled with comfort, sophistication, and personalized attention.

Boutique Stays

For travelers seeking character, personalized service, and a touch of local flavor, Malta's boutique hotels offer a delightful alternative to larger chains. This guide highlights some of the best boutique stays across the islands, helping you find the perfect base for your Maltese adventure.

Valletta & Floriana:

- **Casa Ellul (Valletta)**: Housed in a beautifully restored 19th-century palazzo, Casa Ellul seamlessly blends historic elegance with modern comforts. Each suite is uniquely designed, showcasing original architectural features like Maltese balconies and patterned tiles. A rooftop terrace offers panoramic city views. Its central Valletta location puts you steps from major attractions, restaurants, and bars.
    - Address: 81 Old Bakery Street, Valletta VLT 1452, Malta
    - Distinctive Features: Historic palazzo, individually designed suites, rooftop terrace.
    - Ambiance: Elegant, intimate, luxurious.
    - Location Advantages: Heart of Valletta, close to St. John's Co-Cathedral, Grand Master's Palace, and Upper Barrakka Gardens.
- **The Snop House (Valletta)**: This stylish boutique hotel offers a contemporary take on Maltese hospitality. The rooms are chic and comfortable, featuring modern amenities and tasteful décor. A rooftop terrace provides stunning views of the Grand Harbour. Its location in Valletta offers easy access to the city's cultural attractions and vibrant nightlife.
    - Address: 17 St. Ursula Street, Valletta, VLT 1241, Malta
    - Distinctive Features: Contemporary design, rooftop terrace with harbour views.
    - Ambiance: Stylish, modern, relaxed.
    - Location Advantages: Central Valletta location, near the Valletta Waterfront and Lower Barrakka Gardens.

Mdina & Rabat:

- **The Xara Palace Relais & Chateaux (Mdina)**: Nestled within the ancient walls of Mdina, this 17th-century palace offers a truly luxurious and unique experience. Its elegant rooms and suites feature period furnishings, offering a glimpse into Malta's noble past. Fine dining restaurants and a tranquil courtyard enhance the experience.
    - Address: Triq Il-Kwartier, Mdina MDN 1075, Malta
    - Distinctive Features: Historic palace setting, period furnishings, fine dining.
    - Ambiance: Luxurious, romantic, historic.
    - Location Advantages: Within the walls of Mdina, offering a peaceful and immersive experience.

Gozo:

- **Santa Lucia Boutique Hotel (Santa Lucija, Gozo)**: Located in the tranquil village of Santa Lucija, this boutique hotel offers a peaceful retreat. Its stylish rooms blend traditional Gozitan architecture with modern comforts. A rooftop terrace provides panoramic views of the surrounding countryside. The quiet village setting offers a relaxing escape from the busier parts of Gozo.
    - Address: 10 Triq il-Kappillan, Santa Luċija, Gozo, GŻR 1020, Malta
    - Distinctive Features: Traditional Gozitan architecture, rooftop terrace, tranquil setting.
    - Ambiance: Relaxed, charming, authentic.
    - Location Advantages: Quiet village setting in Gozo, close to Ggantija Temples and other Gozo attractions.

Choosing Your Perfect Boutique Stay:

Consider these factors when choosing your boutique accommodation:

- Location: Choose a location that suits your interests – historical cities, coastal areas, or the tranquil countryside.
- Ambiance: Select a hotel that matches your preferred style – elegant and luxurious, modern and chic, or rustic and charming.
- Amenities: Consider the amenities that are important to you – rooftop terraces, spas, on-site restaurants.
- Nearby Attractions: Check the proximity to the attractions you plan to visit.
- Reviews: Read reviews from other travelers to get insights into their experiences.

By considering these factors and exploring the options above, you can find the perfect boutique stay to enhance your Maltese getaway and create lasting memories.

Budget-Friendly Stays

Traveling to Malta doesn't have to break the bank. The islands offer a range of budget-friendly accommodations that provide comfortable stays without sacrificing location or convenience. This guide highlights some top recommendations for value-conscious travelers.

Hostels:

- **Valletta Backpackers (Valletta)**: Located in the heart of Valletta, this hostel offers dorm rooms and private rooms at affordable rates. It features a communal kitchen, lounge area, and rooftop terrace with city views. Its central location provides easy access to Valletta's attractions and public transport.

- Address: 156 St. Lucia Street, Valletta, VLT 1185, Malta
- Room Rates: Dorm beds from €20-€30 per night, private rooms from €50-€70.
- Amenities: Communal kitchen, lounge, rooftop terrace, free Wi-Fi.
- Location Advantages: Central Valletta location, close to major attractions and bus terminus.

- **Two Pillows Hostel (Sliema)**: Located in the popular seaside town of Sliema, this hostel offers a social atmosphere with dorm rooms and private rooms. It features a common area, kitchen, and a rooftop terrace with sea views. Its proximity to the Sliema promenade and ferry connections makes it a convenient base for exploring the islands.
  - Address: 117 High Street, Sliema, SLM 1543, Malta
  - Room Rates: Dorm beds from €18-€28 per night, private rooms from €45-€65.
  - Amenities: Communal kitchen, common area, rooftop terrace, free Wi-Fi.
  - Location Advantages: Sliema promenade location, close to shops, restaurants, and ferry connections.

Guesthouses and Budget Hotels:

- **Sliema Hotel by ST Hotels (Sliema)**: Offers simple but clean and comfortable rooms at reasonable prices. Its location in Sliema provides easy access to shops, restaurants, and the waterfront.
  - Address: 129 Tower Road, Sliema, SLM 1605, Malta
  - Room Rates: Double rooms from €50-€80 per night.
  - Amenities: Basic amenities, breakfast available, Wi-Fi.

- o Location Advantages: Central Sliema location, close to the promenade and shopping areas.
- **The British Hotel (Valletta)**: Located near the Upper Barrakka Gardens in Valletta, this hotel offers basic but clean rooms at budget-friendly prices. Its central location makes it easy to explore the capital city.
  - o Address: 40 Battery Street, Valletta, VLT 1221, Malta
  - o Room Rates: Double rooms from €40-€70 per night.
  - o Amenities: Basic amenities, breakfast available, Wi-Fi.
  - o Location Advantages: Central Valletta location near major attractions.

Tips for Budget Travelers:

- Travel in the shoulder seasons (spring or autumn): You'll find lower prices and fewer crowds.
- Book in advance, especially during peak season: This will help you secure the best deals.
- Consider self-catering apartments or guesthouses with kitchen facilities: This can help you save money on food.
- Utilize public transportation: Malta's bus network is efficient and affordable.
- Take advantage of free activities: Explore the historic cities, walk along the coast, and visit free museums and gardens.

These budget-friendly stays offer excellent value for money, providing comfortable accommodation in convenient locations without compromising your travel budget. By considering these options and following the tips above, you can enjoy a fantastic trip to Malta without breaking the bank.

Vacation Rentals

Vacation rentals in Malta offer an ideal combination of comfort, privacy, and local charm. Whether you're seeking a cozy retreat for two, a family-friendly villa, or a spacious property for a group, these options cater to diverse needs while providing unique features and memorable experiences.

Valletta Dream Apartments – Valletta

- Location: Various addresses in the heart of Valletta, near landmarks like St. John's Co-Cathedral and the Grandmaster's Palace.
- Accommodation Types: Stylish one- and two-bedroom apartments, perfect for couples or small families.
- Amenities: Modern kitchens, balconies with city views, and free Wi-Fi. Some units feature rooftop terraces for sunset dining.
- Nearby Attractions: Steps away from Valletta's museums, restaurants, and bustling markets.
- Special Features: Immersive Old Town experience with contemporary comforts, ideal for culture enthusiasts and city explorers.

Dar Ta' Żeppi – Gozo

- Location: 36 Triq Ta' Bullara, Qala, Gozo, a peaceful village setting.
- Accommodation Types: A charming farmhouse with multiple rooms and a private pool, suitable for families or groups.
- Amenities: Fully equipped kitchen, BBQ area, garden, and poolside loungers.
- Nearby Attractions: Close to the Blue Lagoon, the Gozo Ferry Terminal, and hiking trails.

- Special Features: Authentic Gozitan architecture with modern updates, offering a serene getaway with plenty of outdoor space for relaxation.

Spinola Bay Sea View Apartments – St. Julian's

- Location: Overlooking Spinola Bay, known for its vibrant nightlife and restaurants.
- Accommodation Types: Contemporary one- to three-bedroom apartments with sea-facing balconies.
- Amenities: Fully equipped kitchens, air conditioning, free parking, and proximity to public transport.
- Nearby Attractions: Spinola Bay promenade, sandy beaches, and the Paceville nightlife district.
- Special Features: Panoramic bay views and easy access to dining and entertainment, making it ideal for couples or groups of friends.

Ta' Rena Farmhouse – Żebbuġ

- Location: Żebbuġ, Gozo, in a picturesque rural setting.
- Accommodation Types: A three-bedroom farmhouse with traditional stone walls and vaulted ceilings.
- Amenities: Private pool, fireplace, large kitchen, and outdoor dining area.
- Nearby Attractions: Close to Ramla Bay, Ġgantija Temples, and local wineries.
- Special Features: A perfect blend of rustic charm and modern comfort, great for families or small groups seeking tranquility.

Mdina View Townhouse – Mdina

- Location: Adjacent to Mdina's historic city walls, offering a unique vantage point of the "Silent City."
- Accommodation Types: A luxurious two-bedroom townhouse with a rooftop terrace.
- Amenities: Stylish interiors, fully equipped kitchen, and panoramic rooftop views.
- Nearby Attractions: Mdina's historic sites, Rabat's catacombs, and quaint local cafes.
- Special Features: Romantic ambiance and a prime location for exploring Malta's history.

These vacation rentals provide flexibility, charm, and convenience, making them excellent choices for travelers seeking a home away from home in Malta.

Practical Accommodation Tips

Finding the right accommodation is crucial for a successful trip to Malta. This guide offers actionable advice for smart travelers, catering to various preferences, budgets, and travel styles.

1. Choosing the Right Type of Accommodation:

- Hotels: Offer a range of services and amenities, suitable for those seeking convenience and comfort. Consider boutique hotels for a more personalized experience.
- Guesthouses & B&Bs: Provide a more intimate and local experience, often at lower prices than hotels.
- Hostels: Ideal for budget travelers and solo adventurers, offering dorm rooms and communal areas.

- Vacation Rentals (Apartments/Villas/Farmhouses): Offer more space, privacy, and self-catering facilities, suitable for families, groups, or longer stays.

2. Finding the Best Deals:

- Travel in the Shoulder Seasons (Spring/Autumn): Enjoy lower prices and fewer crowds compared to the peak summer season.
- Book in Advance: Especially during peak season, booking early can secure better rates and availability.
- Compare Prices Online: Use comparison websites (e.g., Booking.com, Expedia, Hotels.com) to find the best deals.
- Consider Package Deals: Sometimes booking flights and accommodation together can offer cost savings.
- Look for Special Offers and Promotions: Many hotels and rentals offer discounts for longer stays, early bookings, or off-season travel.
- Consider Location Outside Main Tourist Hubs: Staying in quieter towns or villages can offer lower prices.

3. Understanding Booking Policies:

- Check Cancellation Policies: Pay close attention to cancellation policies before booking, especially for non-refundable rates.
- Read the Fine Print: Understand the terms and conditions, including check-in/check-out times, payment methods, and any extra fees.
- Confirm Your Booking: Always confirm your booking directly with the accommodation provider.

4. Maximizing Amenities:

- Take Advantage of Free Amenities: Many accommodations offer free Wi-Fi, breakfast, and other amenities.
- Inquire About Additional Services: Ask about additional services such as airport transfers, laundry service, or local tours.
- Utilize Kitchen Facilities: If staying in a self-catering apartment or guesthouse, make use of the kitchen to save money on dining out.

5. Ensuring Safety and Security:

- Choose Reputable Accommodations: Read reviews from other travelers to get an idea of the accommodation's reputation.
- Secure Your Valuables: Use in-room safes or secure your belongings in a safe place.
- Be Aware of Your Surroundings: Be mindful of your surroundings, especially in unfamiliar areas.

6. Making the Most of Your Accommodation Experience:

- Interact with Staff: Hotel or guesthouse staff can offer valuable local tips and recommendations.
- Explore the Neighborhood: Take time to explore the local area and discover hidden gems.
- Relax and Enjoy Your Stay: Your accommodation should be a place to relax and recharge after a day of exploring.

Tailoring to Different Travel Styles:

- Budget Travelers: Hostels, budget hotels, and self-catering apartments offer the best value.
- Families: Vacation rentals with multiple bedrooms and kitchen facilities are ideal.

- Couples: Boutique hotels or romantic guesthouses offer a more intimate experience.
- Solo Travelers: Hostels or centrally located guesthouses provide opportunities to meet other travelers.

By following these practical tips, you can find the perfect accommodation to enhance your Maltese getaway, regardless of your budget or travel style, ensuring a comfortable, safe, and rewarding experience.

CHAPTER FIVE

Exploring Malta

Top Destinations

Valletta: The Capital City

Valletta, Malta's captivating capital, stands as a testament to the island's rich and layered history. This UNESCO World Heritage city, built by the Knights of St. John after the Great Siege of 1565, is a living museum of Baroque architecture, imposing fortifications, and vibrant cultural life. Compact yet brimming with attractions, Valletta offers a unique and unforgettable experience.

A City Forged in History:

Valletta's story is inextricably linked to the Knights of St. John, a Roman Catholic military order. Grand Master Jean Parisot de Valette laid the foundation stone in 1566, envisioning a fortified city that would withstand future invasions. The city's grid layout, designed by the Italian military engineer Francesco Laparelli, was revolutionary for its time, allowing for efficient movement of troops and artillery.

Key Attractions - A Journey Through Time:

- St. John's Co-Cathedral: This opulent cathedral is a masterpiece of Baroque art and architecture. Its interior is adorned with intricate carvings, gilded decorations, and stunning frescoes by Mattia Preti. The highlight is Caravaggio's masterpiece, "The Beheading of St. John the Baptist," a powerful and moving work of art.
- Grand Master's Palace: Formerly the seat of the Knights of St. John and later the residence of British governors, this palace

now houses the Office of the President of Malta. Its impressive state rooms, courtyards, and armoury offer a glimpse into Malta's past.
- Upper Barrakka Gardens: Perched on the city's bastions, these gardens offer breathtaking panoramic views of the Grand Harbour and the Three Cities. The Saluting Battery, located below the gardens, fires cannons daily at noon and 4 pm.
- Lower Barrakka Gardens: A smaller and more tranquil garden, featuring a neoclassical monument dedicated to Sir Alexander Ball. It provides stunning views of the sea and the surrounding fortifications.
- National Museum of Archaeology: Housed in the Auberge de Provence, this museum showcases Malta's rich prehistoric heritage, with artifacts dating back to the Neolithic period.
- Teatru Manoel: One of Europe's oldest working theatres, this beautifully preserved theatre hosts a variety of performances throughout the year.

Exploring the City:

- Walking the Streets: Valletta's grid layout makes it easy to navigate. Simply wander through its narrow streets, admiring the Baroque architecture, colourful balconies, and historic buildings.
- Republic Street: The city's main thoroughfare, lined with shops, cafes, and restaurants.
- Merchant Street: A bustling street market offering a variety of goods.
- Strait Street: Once known for its lively nightlife, now home to a variety of bars and restaurants.

Practical Information:

- How to Get There: Valletta is easily accessible by bus from all over Malta. Ferry services connect Valletta to Sliema and the Three Cities.
- Best Time to Visit: Valletta can be visited year-round, but spring (April-May) and autumn (September-October) offer pleasant weather and fewer crowds.

Tips for Visitors:

- Wear comfortable shoes, as the city's streets are paved with uneven cobblestones.
- Visit St. John's Co-Cathedral early in the morning to avoid crowds.
- Take a walk along the city walls for stunning views.
- Enjoy a traditional Maltese meal at one of the many restaurants.
- Take a harbour cruise for a different perspective of the city.

Valletta is more than just a capital city; it's a living, breathing testament to Malta's rich history and vibrant culture. By exploring its streets, visiting its historical sites, and immersing yourself in its atmosphere, you can experience the unique charm of this remarkable city.

Mdina: The Silent City

Perched on a hilltop in the heart of Malta, Mdina, often referred to as the "Silent City," offers a captivating journey into the island's rich history. As the old capital of Malta, Mdina boasts a fascinating past, dating back over 4,000 years. Its narrow, winding streets, imposing fortifications, and stunning views create a unique and enchanting atmosphere.

A History Etched in Stone:

Mdina's history is a tapestry woven with threads of Phoenician, Roman, Arab, and Norman influences. Originally settled by the Phoenicians around 700 BC, the city was later fortified by the Romans and served as their capital, known as Melite. After Arab rule, the Normans further fortified the city, giving it its present medieval character. When the Knights of St. John arrived in 1530, they established their capital in Birgu (Vittoriosa), leading to Mdina's gradual decline and its nickname, "The Silent City."

Key Attractions - Echoes of the Past:

- Mdina Cathedral: Dedicated to St. Paul, this Baroque cathedral stands on the site of a former Roman temple and later a Norman church. Its impressive facade and ornate interior are testaments to Malta's rich religious heritage.
- Mdina Dungeons: Located beneath the Vilhena Palace, these dungeons offer a chilling glimpse into the city's darker past, with exhibits showcasing medieval torture methods and prison life.
- Vilhena Palace: Built in the 18th century by Grand Master António Manoel de Vilhena, this imposing palace now houses the National Museum of Natural History. Its elegant architecture and courtyard are worth exploring.
- City Walls and Bastions: Mdina's fortified walls offer breathtaking panoramic views of the island, stretching as far as the sea. Walking along the ramparts is a must for any visitor.
- Palazzo Falson Historic House Museum: This well-preserved medieval palace offers a fascinating insight into the life of a wealthy Maltese noble family. Its collection of antique furniture, art, and artifacts provides a glimpse into the past.

Exploring the City:

- Walking the Silent Streets: Mdina's narrow, winding streets are best explored on foot. Take your time to wander through the car-free alleys, admiring the historic architecture and soaking up the peaceful atmosphere.
- Main Gate: The imposing main gate, featured in the popular TV series "Game of Thrones," is a striking entrance to the city.
- St. Paul's Square: The main square in Mdina, home to the Mdina Cathedral and other historic buildings.

Practical Information:

- How to Get There: Mdina is easily accessible by bus from Valletta and other parts of Malta. There are also taxi services available.
- Best Time to Visit: Mdina can be visited year-round, but it's best to avoid midday during the hot summer months. Early mornings and late afternoons offer a more pleasant experience.

Tips for Visitors:

- Wear comfortable shoes for walking on uneven surfaces.
- Respect the quiet atmosphere of the city.
- Visit early in the morning or late in the afternoon to avoid crowds.
- Enjoy a leisurely meal or a coffee at one of the cafes or restaurants within the city walls.
- Combine your visit with a trip to nearby Rabat, which offers further historical and cultural attractions.

Mdina is a truly unique destination, offering a step back in time and a glimpse into Malta's rich history. Its peaceful atmosphere, stunning architecture, and panoramic views make it a must-visit for anyone traveling to Malta.

Sliema and St. Julian's

Sliema and St. Julian's, nestled side-by-side along Malta's northeastern coast, represent the modern face of the island. These bustling towns offer a vibrant mix of shopping, dining, entertainment, and beach life, attracting both locals and tourists seeking a lively and cosmopolitan atmosphere. Once quiet fishing villages, they have transformed into thriving commercial and tourist centers, offering a dynamic contrast to Malta's historic cities.

Sliema: Shopping and Promenade Life:

Sliema, meaning "peace" or "comfort," is known for its long promenade stretching along the coastline, offering stunning views of Valletta across Marsamxett Harbour. This promenade is the heart of Sliema, a hub of activity with locals jogging, strolling, and socializing.

- Key Attractions:
    - Sliema Promenade: This scenic promenade is perfect for leisurely walks, offering stunning sea views and access to rocky beaches and swimming spots.
    - Shopping: Sliema is a shopper's paradise, with a wide variety of shops, from high-street brands to local boutiques, concentrated along Tower Road and Bisazza Street.
    - Tigné Point: A modern development with upscale shops, restaurants, and residential apartments, offering a contemporary urban experience.
    - Exiles Beach: A popular rocky beach with clear waters, ideal for swimming and sunbathing.

- Activities: Shopping, walking along the promenade, swimming, sunbathing, boat trips to Valletta and other destinations.
- Dining: Sliema offers a diverse culinary scene, with restaurants serving everything from traditional Maltese cuisine to international fare.
- How to Get There: Easily accessible by bus from Valletta and other parts of Malta. Ferry connections to Valletta.
- Best Time to Visit: Year-round, but summer is ideal for beach activities.

St. Julian's: Entertainment and Nightlife:

St. Julian's, just east of Sliema, is known for its lively atmosphere, particularly its nightlife hub in Paceville. This area is packed with bars, clubs, and restaurants, attracting a younger crowd.

- Key Attractions:
    - Spinola Bay: A picturesque bay with colourful fishing boats (luzzus), lined with restaurants and cafes.
    - Paceville: Malta's main nightlife district, offering a wide variety of bars, clubs, and entertainment venues.
    - Portomaso Marina: An upscale marina with luxury apartments, a hotel, and high-end restaurants.
    - St. George's Bay: A sandy beach popular for swimming and sunbathing.
- Activities: Nightlife, dining, swimming, sunbathing, water sports.
- Dining: St. Julian's boasts a wide range of restaurants, from casual eateries to fine dining establishments.
- How to Get There: Easily accessible by bus from Valletta and other parts of Malta. Walking distance from Sliema.
- Best Time to Visit: Summer for beach activities and nightlife, year-round for dining and entertainment.

Sliema and St. Julian's - A Combined Experience:

These two towns seamlessly blend into each other, offering a diverse range of experiences within easy reach.

- Walking Between the Towns: The promenade connects Sliema and St. Julian's, making it easy to walk between the two towns and enjoy the coastal scenery.
- Combining Activities: You can easily combine shopping in Sliema with a relaxing afternoon on the beach in St. Julian's or a night out in Paceville.

Tips for Visitors:

- Be prepared for crowds, especially during the summer months.
- If you're looking for a quieter experience, consider staying in the quieter parts of Sliema or further away from Paceville in St. Julian's.
- Take a boat trip from Sliema or St. Julian's to explore the coastline or visit other parts of Malta.
- Enjoy the diverse culinary scene, from traditional Maltese cuisine to international flavors.

Sliema and St. Julian's offer a vibrant and modern experience in Malta, providing a contrast to the island's historic cities and offering a wide range of activities and entertainment options. Whether you're looking for shopping, dining, nightlife, or beach life, you'll find it in these bustling coastal towns.

The Three Cities: Vittoriosa, Senglea, and Cospicua

Across the Grand Harbour from Valletta lie the Three Cities: Vittoriosa (Birgu), Senglea (Isla), and Cospicua (Bormla). These fortified cities offer a captivating journey into Malta's maritime heart, revealing a rich tapestry of history, culture, and authentic local life.

Older than Valletta, they played a crucial role in Malta's defense and development, offering a more intimate and less crowded experience compared to the capital.

A Shared History of Resilience:

The Three Cities have a long and intertwined history, deeply connected to the sea and Malta's strategic importance. They provided shelter to various settlers throughout the centuries and were at the forefront of major historical events, including the Great Siege of 1565. The Knights of St. John first settled in Birgu upon their arrival in Malta, making it the initial base of their operations before moving to Valletta.

Vittoriosa (Birgu): The Oldest City:

Vittoriosa, also known as Birgu, is the oldest of the Three Cities and boasts a rich maritime heritage. Its narrow, winding streets, historic palaces, and imposing fort offer a fascinating glimpse into Malta's past.

- Key Attractions:
    - Fort St. Angelo: This imposing fort played a crucial role in the Great Siege of 1565. Its strategic location at the tip of the peninsula offers stunning views of the Grand Harbour.
    - Inquisitor's Palace: One of the few remaining Inquisitor's palaces in Europe, this museum offers a chilling insight into the history of the Inquisition in Malta.
    - Malta Maritime Museum: Located in the former British Naval Bakery, this museum showcases Malta's long maritime history.
    - Birgu Waterfront: A picturesque waterfront area lined with restaurants and cafes.

- Activities: Exploring the historic fort and palaces, visiting museums, enjoying waterfront dining, taking a dghajsa boat trip.

Senglea (Isla): The Watchtower:

Senglea, also known as Isla, is the smallest of the Three Cities. Its strategic location on a peninsula provided excellent vantage points for observing the Grand Harbour.

- Key Attractions:
    - Senglea Point (Gardjola Gardens): Offering panoramic views of the Grand Harbour and Valletta, this is a popular spot for photos. The iconic gardjola (watchtower) with its carved symbols is a prominent landmark.
    - St. Philip's Church: A historic church with a beautiful interior.
- Activities: Enjoying panoramic views, exploring the narrow streets, visiting the church.

Cospicua (Bormla): The Newest City:

Cospicua, also known as Bormla, is the largest of the Three Cities. It developed later than Birgu and Senglea and served as a vital part of the fortifications surrounding the Grand Harbour.

- Key Attractions:
    - Cottonera Lines: A series of fortifications built to protect the Three Cities.
    - Parish Church of the Immaculate Conception: A beautiful church with an impressive dome.
- Activities: Exploring the fortifications, visiting the church.

Exploring the Three Cities:

- Walking: The best way to explore the Three Cities is on foot. Their narrow streets and historic alleyways are perfect for leisurely strolls.
- Dghajsa Boat Trips: Take a traditional dghajsa boat trip across the Grand Harbour for a unique perspective of the cities and Valletta.
- Combined Visit: The Three Cities are easily explored in a single day, offering a rewarding experience for history and culture enthusiasts.

Practical Information:

- How to Get There: Ferry connections from Valletta. Bus services from other parts of Malta.
- Best Time to Visit: Year-round.
- Tips for Visitors:
    - Wear comfortable shoes for walking on uneven surfaces.
    - Take a dghajsa boat trip for a unique perspective.
    - Combine your visit with a trip to Valletta.
    - Enjoy a meal at one of the waterfront restaurants.

The Three Cities offer a captivating journey into Malta's maritime past, providing a more authentic and intimate experience compared to the bustling capital. By exploring these historic cities, you can discover the heart and soul of Malta.

Gozo Island

Gozo, Malta's sister island, offers a distinct contrast to the mainland. With its rolling hills, picturesque villages, and rugged coastline, Gozo exudes a tranquil and laid-back atmosphere. This idyllic island is a haven for those seeking a peaceful escape, offering a blend of natural beauty, historical sites, and authentic local charm.

A Landscape of Natural Beauty:

Gozo's landscape is characterized by its fertile valleys, terraced fields, and dramatic cliffs that plunge into the azure Mediterranean Sea. The island's natural beauty provides a stunning backdrop for outdoor activities and exploration.

Key Attractions - From Ancient Wonders to Coastal Gems:

- Victoria (Rabat): Gozo's capital city, Victoria, is a charming hub of local life. Its heart is Independence Square (It-Tokk), a bustling market square surrounded by cafes and shops. The imposing Citadella, a fortified city within Victoria, offers panoramic views of the island.
- Citadella: This ancient fortified city, perched on a hilltop in Victoria, has a rich history dating back to the Bronze Age. Its impressive walls, historic buildings, and stunning views make it a must-visit.
- Ggantija Temples: These megalithic temples, dating back to around 3600-3200 BC, are among the oldest free-standing structures in the world. They offer a fascinating glimpse into Gozo's prehistoric past.
- Dwejra Bay: Located on the west coast, Dwejra Bay is a dramatic coastal landscape. While the iconic Azure Window collapsed in 2017, the area still offers stunning natural features, including the Inland Sea, a saltwater lagoon connected to the sea by a narrow tunnel, and the Blue Hole, a popular diving spot.

- Ramla Bay: Gozo's most popular beach, Ramla Bay, is known for its distinctive red sand and clear blue waters. It's an ideal spot for swimming, sunbathing, and relaxing.
- Salt Pans: The coastal areas of Gozo feature unique salt pans, carved into the rock formations. These traditional salt-harvesting sites are a testament to Gozo's history and culture.

Exploring Gozo:

- By Car or Scooter: Renting a car or scooter offers the most flexibility for exploring Gozo's diverse landscapes and reaching remote areas.
- By Bus: Gozo has a public bus network that connects the main towns and villages.
- By Bicycle: Cycling is a popular way to explore Gozo, offering a more active and immersive experience.
- Walking and Hiking: Gozo offers several scenic walking and hiking trails, allowing you to appreciate the island's natural beauty at your own pace.

Activities in Gozo:

- Swimming and Sunbathing: Enjoy the crystal-clear waters and sandy beaches of Ramla Bay, Marsalforn Bay, and Xlendi Bay.
- Diving and Snorkeling: Explore the underwater world at popular dive sites like the Blue Hole and the Inland Sea.
- Hiking and Walking: Discover the island's scenic trails and enjoy panoramic views.
- Visiting Historical Sites: Explore the Citadella, Ggantija Temples, and other historical landmarks.
- Enjoying Local Cuisine: Sample traditional Gozitan dishes at local restaurants.

Practical Information:

- How to Get There: The main way to reach Gozo is by ferry from Ċirkewwa on Malta's northern coast. The ferry journey takes approximately 25 minutes. There is also a fast ferry service from Valletta to Gozo.
- Best Time to Visit: Gozo can be visited year-round. Spring and autumn offer pleasant weather for outdoor activities, while summer is ideal for beach holidays.

Tips for Visitors:

- Rent a car or scooter for maximum flexibility.
- Explore the Citadella in Victoria for panoramic views.
- Visit the Ggantija Temples to experience Gozo's ancient history.
- Relax on the red sands of Ramla Bay.
- Take a boat trip to explore the coastline and nearby islands.

Gozo offers a tranquil and authentic Maltese experience, providing a welcome escape from the hustle and bustle of the mainland. With its stunning natural beauty, rich history, and laid-back atmosphere, Gozo is a must-visit destination for anyone traveling to the Maltese Islands.

Comino and the Blue Lagoon

Comino, the smallest inhabited island of the Maltese archipelago, is a true gem of the Mediterranean. Its name derives from the cumin herb that once grew abundantly on the island. While sparsely populated, Comino draws visitors from far and wide with its breathtaking natural beauty, most notably the iconic Blue Lagoon. This guide delves into the wonders of Comino and provides practical information for planning your visit.

The Blue Lagoon: A Natural Wonder:

The Blue Lagoon is Comino's crown jewel, a stunning bay nestled between Comino and the smaller islet of Cominotto. Its shallow, turquoise waters and white sandy seabed create a picture-perfect scene reminiscent of a tropical paradise. The lagoon's crystal-clear waters are ideal for swimming, snorkeling, and simply relaxing in this idyllic setting.

Key Attractions and Activities:

- Swimming and Sunbathing: The Blue Lagoon's calm and shallow waters are perfect for swimming and paddling. The surrounding rocks provide ample space for sunbathing.
- Snorkeling and Diving: The clear waters of the Blue Lagoon offer excellent visibility for snorkeling and diving. Explore the diverse marine life and underwater rock formations.
- Santa Marija Tower: This historic watchtower, built in the 17th century by the Knights of St. John, stands guard over Comino. It offers panoramic views of the island and the surrounding sea.
- Comino's Hiking Trails: Comino offers several scenic hiking trails that allow you to explore the island's rugged landscape and discover hidden coves and bays.
- Other Beaches and Bays: While the Blue Lagoon is the most famous, Comino has other beautiful beaches and bays, such as Santa Marija Bay and San Niklaw Bay, which offer a quieter alternative.

Practical Information:

- How to Get There:
  - Ferries: Regular ferry services operate to Comino from Ċirkewwa on Malta's northern coast and from Mġarr on Gozo.
  - Boat Tours: Many boat tours from Malta and Gozo include a stop at the Blue Lagoon, often combining it with visits to other attractions.
- Best Time to Visit:
  - Summer (June-August): The best time for swimming and sunbathing, but also the busiest time.
  - Shoulder Seasons (April-May & September-October): Offer pleasant weather and fewer crowds.
- Facilities:
  - Limited Facilities: Comino has limited facilities. There are some food and drink vendors at the Blue Lagoon, but it's advisable to bring your own food and drinks, especially if you're on a budget.
  - Sunbeds and Umbrellas: Sunbeds and umbrellas are available for rent at the Blue Lagoon, but they can be expensive and get booked quickly during peak season.
  - No Accommodation: There is only one hotel on Comino, so most visitors visit on a day trip.

Tips for Visitors:

- Arrive Early: The Blue Lagoon gets very crowded, especially during the summer months. Arriving early in the morning will allow you to enjoy the lagoon before the crowds arrive.
- Bring Essentials: Bring sunscreen, a hat, sunglasses, and a towel.

- Wear Appropriate Footwear: The rocks around the Blue Lagoon can be sharp, so wearing appropriate footwear is recommended.
- Bring Cash: Many vendors on Comino do not accept credit cards.
- Respect the Environment: Keep the island clean and avoid littering.

Beyond the Blue Lagoon:

While the Blue Lagoon is the main attraction, Comino has much more to offer. Take the time to explore the island's hiking trails, discover hidden coves, and visit the historic Santa Marija Tower.

Comino and the Blue Lagoon offer a truly unforgettable experience, a paradise of turquoise waters and natural beauty. By planning your visit carefully and following these tips, you can make the most of your time on this stunning island.

Marsaxlokk and its Fishing Village Charm

Nestled in the southeastern part of Malta, Marsaxlokk is a picturesque fishing village that offers a charming glimpse into traditional Maltese life. Its name, a combination of "Marsa" (port) and "Xlokk" (south wind), reflects its close relationship with the sea. Renowned for its colorful fishing boats, bustling Sunday fish market, and laid-back atmosphere, Marsaxlokk provides a delightful escape from the more tourist-heavy areas of Malta.

A Harbour of Colourful Traditions:

Marsaxlokk's harbor is its defining feature, dotted with brightly painted traditional fishing boats known as luzzus. These boats, adorned with the iconic "eyes of Osiris" believed to protect fishermen at sea, create a vibrant and photogenic scene. The village's economy revolves around fishing, and the daily catch provides fresh seafood for the local restaurants.

Key Attractions and Activities:

- o Marsaxlokk Bay: The heart of the village, the bay is a bustling hub of activity with fishermen bringing in their daily catch, locals strolling along the waterfront, and tourists admiring the colorful luzzus.
- o Sunday Fish Market: This bustling market is a must-visit for seafood lovers. Local fishermen sell their fresh catch, offering a wide variety of fish and shellfish. The market also features stalls selling local produce, honey, and other Maltese products.
- o Waterfront Promenade: A pleasant promenade stretches along the harbor, lined with restaurants and cafes offering stunning views of the bay.
- o Parish Church of Our Lady of Pompeii: A beautiful church located in the village center.
- o St. Peter's Pool: A natural rock pool located a short distance from Marsaxlokk, popular for swimming and sunbathing (accessible by boat or a short walk).
- o Fort St. Lucian: A historic fort located on the headland overlooking Marsaxlokk Bay.

Experiencing Marsaxlokk:

- o Enjoy Fresh Seafood: Marsaxlokk is renowned for its fresh seafood restaurants. Enjoy a delicious meal overlooking the harbor, savoring the flavors of the Mediterranean.
- o Explore the Market: Wander through the Sunday fish market or the daily market for local produce and souvenirs.
- o Take a Boat Trip: Take a boat trip to St. Peter's Pool or explore the coastline from the sea.

- Relax and Soak Up the Atmosphere: Marsaxlokk offers a relaxed and laid-back atmosphere. Take your time to stroll along the waterfront, watch the fishermen at work, and enjoy the local life.

Practical Information:

- How to Get There:
    - Bus: Regular bus services connect Marsaxlokk to Valletta and other parts of Malta.
    - Car: Marsaxlokk is easily accessible by car. However, parking can be challenging, especially on Sundays during the market.
- Best Time to Visit:
    - Sunday: For the bustling fish market.
    - Year-round: For enjoying the picturesque harbor and fresh seafood.
- Tips for Visitors:
    - Arrive early on Sunday to experience the fish market at its busiest.
    - Be prepared for crowds on Sundays.
    - Bargaining is acceptable at the market.
    - Try some local Maltese delicacies, such as lampuki pie (seasonal).

Marsaxlokk offers a unique and authentic Maltese experience, providing a glimpse into the island's fishing traditions and laid-back coastal lifestyle. Its colorful harbor, fresh seafood, and welcoming atmosphere make it a must-visit destination for anyone traveling to Malta.

Beaches and Swimming Spots

Malta's coastline is a mosaic of golden sands, dramatic cliffs, and crystal-clear waters, offering a diverse range of beaches and swimming spots to suit every taste. Whether you're seeking a lively beach with ample amenities or a secluded cove for a tranquil escape, Malta has something for you.

Sandy Beaches: Golden Shores and Family Fun

- Mellieħa Bay (Għadira Bay): Malta's largest sandy beach, Mellieħa Bay, is a haven for families. Its shallow, calm waters are perfect for children, and the long stretch of golden sand offers plenty of space for sunbathing and building sandcastles. Amenities include sunbeds, umbrellas, water sports rentals (pedalos, kayaks, windsurfing), and numerous cafes and restaurants nearby. Easily accessible by bus and car with ample parking.
    - Best for: Families, water sports enthusiasts.
- Golden Bay: This picturesque bay on the northwest coast is known for its fine golden sand and stunning views. It's a popular spot for swimming, sunbathing, and enjoying the sunset. Facilities include sunbeds, umbrellas, a beach bar, and water sports rentals. Accessible by bus and car with parking available.
    - Best for: Sunbathers, sunset views.
- Għajn Tuffieħa (Riviera Beach): Located next to Golden Bay, Għajn Tuffieħa offers a more secluded and natural setting. Accessed by a set of steps, it tends to be less crowded. It has a more laid-back atmosphere with a small kiosk for refreshments.
    - Best for: Those seeking a quieter beach experience.

- Ramla Bay (Gozo): Gozo's largest sandy beach is famous for its unique reddish-orange sand. Ramla Bay offers a wide expanse of sand, clear blue waters, and a relaxed atmosphere. It has basic amenities like a few kiosks selling refreshments.
    - Best for: Families, those seeking a unique beach experience.

Rocky Beaches and Coves: Secluded Beauty and Snorkeling Hotspots

- St. Peter's Pool: Near Marsaxlokk, this natural rock pool is a favorite among locals and tourists. Its crystal-clear turquoise waters are perfect for swimming, snorkeling, and even cliff jumping (for the adventurous). There are no facilities, so bring your own food, drinks, and shade. Accessible by boat from Marsaxlokk or a short walk.
    - Best for: Snorkeling, cliff jumping (with caution), those seeking a natural swimming spot.
- Blue Lagoon (Comino): This iconic lagoon, located between Comino and Cominotto, is renowned for its incredibly clear turquoise waters and white sandy seabed. It's a paradise for swimming, snorkeling, and photography. Facilities include kiosks selling food and drinks, and sunbeds and umbrellas for rent (can be expensive and crowded in peak season). Accessible by ferry from Ċirkewwa (Malta) and Mġarr (Gozo).
    - Best for: Swimming, snorkeling, photography.
- Ġnejna Bay: This sandy beach nestled among cliffs near Mġarr offers a quieter alternative to the more popular beaches. It's surrounded by countryside and offers a more natural setting. There's a small kiosk for refreshments.
    - Best for: Those seeking a quieter beach experience, nature lovers.

Other Notable Swimming Spots:

- Sliema Front: The long promenade in Sliema offers various rocky swimming spots with easy access to amenities and restaurants.
- St. Julian's Coastline: Similar to Sliema, St. Julian's offers rocky swimming spots, particularly around Spinola Bay and St. George's Bay (which has a small sandy area).
- Xlendi Bay (Gozo): A picturesque bay in Gozo with clear waters, popular for swimming, snorkeling, and diving.

Practical Tips for Beachgoers:

- Sun Protection: The Maltese sun is strong, especially during summer. Use high SPF sunscreen, wear a hat, and seek shade during peak hours.
- Footwear: Wear appropriate footwear, especially for rocky beaches and coves.
- Water Safety: Be aware of currents and only swim in designated areas. Check for any warning flags.
- Jellyfish: Jellyfish can be present in Maltese waters, particularly during certain times of the year. If stung, seek medical advice if necessary.
- Facilities: Check if the beach you're visiting has facilities like restrooms, showers, and lifeguards.
- Best Time to Visit: Summer (June-August) is ideal for beach holidays, but it can be crowded. Shoulder seasons (May-June and September-October) offer pleasant weather and fewer crowds.
- Transportation: Check bus routes and schedules if relying on public transport. Parking can be limited at some beaches, especially during peak season.

Malta's diverse coastline offers a wealth of opportunities for enjoying the Mediterranean Sea. By choosing the right beach or swimming spot and following these practical tips, you can make the most of your seaside experience in Malta.

Popular Outdoor Activities

Malta's stunning natural landscapes, crystal-clear waters, and diverse coastline provide a perfect playground for outdoor enthusiasts. From gentle hikes along scenic trails to thrilling dives into the deep blue, the Maltese Islands offer a wide range of activities to suit all adventure levels and interests. This guide explores the best outdoor experiences Malta has to offer.

Hiking and Walking: Discovering Hidden Gems on Foot

Malta's network of walking trails offers diverse landscapes, from coastal paths with breathtaking sea views to inland routes through valleys and countryside.

- Recommended Locations:
    - Dingli Cliffs: Offering dramatic coastal views and clifftop walks.
    - Coastal paths around Gozo: Explore the rugged coastline and enjoy stunning sea views.
    - Comino: Hike across the island to discover hidden coves and bays.
    - Victoria Lines: A historical defensive line offering scenic walks through the countryside.
- Difficulty Levels: Trails range from easy strolls to more challenging hikes.
- Equipment Needs: Comfortable walking shoes, water, sunscreen, hat.

- Guided Tours: Several companies offer guided hiking tours, providing insights into the local flora, fauna, and history.
- Safety Tips: Stay on marked trails, be aware of uneven terrain, carry sufficient water, and check the weather forecast before setting out.
- Best Time for Hiking: Spring and autumn offer pleasant temperatures for hiking. Avoid midday during the summer heat.

Water Sports: Exploring the Azure Waters

Malta's crystal-clear waters are ideal for a variety of water sports, from relaxing swims to adrenaline-pumping adventures.

- Swimming and Snorkeling:
  - Recommended Locations: Blue Lagoon (Comino), Ramla Bay (Gozo), Golden Bay, Mellieħa Bay, St. Peter's Pool.
  - Equipment Needs: Swimsuit, towel, sunscreen, snorkel gear (optional).
  - Safety Tips: Be aware of currents, check for jellyfish, and swim in designated areas.
- Diving: Malta is a renowned diving destination, offering diverse dive sites, including wrecks, caves, and reefs.
  - Recommended Locations: Blue Hole (Gozo), Inland Sea (Gozo), Um El Faroud wreck, P29 wreck.
  - Equipment Needs: Diving equipment (can be rented), certification required for certain dives.
  - Guided Tours: Numerous dive centers offer courses, guided dives, and equipment rentals.
  - Safety Tips: Dive with a reputable dive center, follow safety guidelines, and be aware of dive conditions.
- Kayaking and Stand-Up Paddleboarding (SUP): Explore the coastline at your own pace and discover hidden coves and bays.

- o Recommended Locations: Numerous bays and inlets around Malta and Gozo.
- o Equipment Needs: Kayak or SUP board, paddle, life jacket.
- o Rentals and Tours: Rentals and guided tours are available at many beaches and water sports centers.
- o Safety Tips: Wear a life jacket, be aware of wind and currents, and stay close to the shore.
- Windsurfing and Kitesurfing: Take advantage of Malta's wind conditions for these thrilling water sports.
  - o Recommended Locations: Mellieħa Bay, Armier Bay.
  - o Equipment Needs: Windsurfing or kitesurfing equipment (can be rented), lessons recommended for beginners.
  - o Rentals and Lessons: Schools and rental centers are available at popular windsurfing and kitesurfing spots.
  - o Safety Tips: Be aware of wind and sea conditions, and have appropriate training.
- Jet Skiing and Boat Rentals: Enjoy the thrill of riding a jet ski or renting a boat to explore the coastline.
  - o Recommended Locations: Many beaches and marinas offer jet ski rentals and boat charters.
  - o Safety Tips: Follow safety guidelines and operate equipment responsibly.

Cycling: Exploring the Islands on Two Wheels

Cycling offers a great way to explore Malta and Gozo at your own pace, discovering hidden villages and scenic routes.

- Recommended Locations:
  - o Gozo: Gozo's quieter roads and rolling hills make it ideal for cycling.

- ○ Coastal roads in less congested areas of Malta: Explore the northern and western coasts of Malta for less traffic.
- Difficulty Levels: Routes range from easy coastal rides to more challenging hill climbs.
- Equipment Needs: Bicycle, helmet, water, sunscreen.
- Rentals: Bike rentals are available in various locations, including Valletta, Sliema, and Gozo.
- Guided Tours: Some companies offer guided cycling tours.
- Safety Tips: Wear a helmet, be visible to traffic, be aware of road conditions, and carry water.

Golfing: A Scenic Round with Mediterranean Views

Malta offers a unique golfing experience with scenic courses overlooking the Mediterranean Sea.

- Royal Malta Golf Club: The main golf course in Malta, offering an 18-hole course with challenging fairways and stunning views.
- Equipment Needs: Golf clubs and appropriate attire.
- Booking: Book tee times in advance.

Boat Tours: Exploring the Coastline from the Sea

Boat tours offer a fantastic way to see Malta's coastline from a different perspective, discovering hidden coves, sea caves, and other scenic spots.

- Types of Tours: Harbour cruises, day trips to Comino and Gozo, sunset cruises, private boat charters.
- Recommended Locations: Tours depart from Valletta, Sliema, Bugibba, and other coastal towns.
- Booking: Book tours in advance, especially during peak season.

Seasonal Factors and Ideal Times:

- Summer (June-August): Ideal for swimming, sunbathing, and water sports.
- Spring (April-May) and Autumn (September-October): Pleasant temperatures for hiking, cycling, and other outdoor activities.
- Winter (November-March): Mild weather, suitable for hiking and exploring historical sites.

Tips for Making the Most of Malta's Outdoor Offerings:

- Plan ahead: Research activities and book tours or rentals in advance, especially during peak season.
- Check the weather forecast: Be prepared for changing weather conditions.
- Wear appropriate clothing and footwear: Dress for the activity and weather.
- Stay hydrated: Drink plenty of water, especially during the summer months.
- Respect the environment: Leave no trace and protect Malta's natural beauty.

Malta's diverse outdoor activities offer something for everyone, from relaxing beach days to thrilling adventures. By planning ahead and taking necessary precautions, you can make the most of your outdoor experience in this beautiful Mediterranean destination.

Wellness and Spas

Malta's tranquil Mediterranean setting makes it an ideal destination for wellness and relaxation. From luxurious hotel spas to intimate day spas, the island offers a diverse range of experiences to revitalize body and soul. This guide highlights some of Malta's top-rated spas and wellness centers, focusing on their unique offerings and practical information.

Luxury Hotel Spas:

- Myoka Spas (Multiple Locations): Myoka operates several award-winning spas across Malta, ensuring a consistent standard of excellence. Key locations include the Hilton Malta (St. Julian's), Salini Resort (Salina Bay), and 66 St. Paul's & Spa (Valletta).
  - Ambiance: Each Myoka spa offers a tranquil and serene atmosphere, designed to promote relaxation and well-being.
  - Signature Services: Extensive massage menu featuring various techniques (including traditional Maltese massage incorporating local olive oil), rejuvenating facials, detoxifying body wraps and scrubs (using ingredients like sea salt and honey), hydrotherapy treatments, and specialized beauty services.
  - Special Features: Depending on the location, facilities may include saunas, steam rooms, Jacuzzis, indoor pools, and dedicated relaxation areas.
  - Practical Information: Pricing varies depending on the location and treatment. Expect luxury spa pricing. Advance booking is essential, especially during peak season. Check their website for special offers, packages, and operating hours.
- The Phoenicia Malta Spa & Wellness (Valletta): Located within the iconic Phoenicia Malta hotel, this spa offers a sophisticated and luxurious escape.
  - Ambiance: Elegant and refined, reflecting the hotel's historic charm and luxurious atmosphere.

- Signature Services: A curated selection of massages, facials, body treatments, and signature rituals focusing on relaxation, rejuvenation, and holistic well-being.
- Special Features: Himalayan salt room, sauna, steam room, experience showers, and a heated indoor pool.
- Practical Information: High-end luxury spa pricing. Advance booking is crucial. Consider combining a spa treatment with a hotel stay for the ultimate indulgent experience. Check their website for pricing, packages, and operating hours.

Day Spas and Wellness Centers:

- Nataraya Day Spa & Wellness (Mellieħa): With locations at the Solana Hotel & Spa and the Pergola Hotel & Spa in Mellieħa, Nataraya focuses on natural and holistic therapies.
  - Ambiance: Tranquil and welcoming, with a focus on creating a relaxing and nurturing environment.
  - Signature Services: A diverse range of massages, facials, body wraps, and specialized treatments, including their signature Seashells Massage.
  - Special Features: Emphasis on using organic and natural products, some sourced locally.
  - Practical Information: Mid-range pricing offering good value. Check their website for special offers, packages, and operating hours.
- Carisma Spa & Wellness (Multiple Locations): With multiple locations across Malta, Carisma offers a convenient and accessible option for various beauty and wellness treatments.
  - Ambiance: Modern and professional, with a focus on providing effective and affordable treatments.
  - Signature Services: Wide range of massages, facials, waxing, and nail services.

- o Special Features: Varies by location.
- o Practical Information: Check their website for locations, pricing, special offers, and operating hours.

Holistic Wellness Experiences:

- Yoga and Meditation Retreats: Numerous studios and retreat centers across Malta offer yoga and meditation classes and retreats. Look for retreats that incorporate local elements, like outdoor yoga sessions with sea views or meditation practices in historical settings.

Tips for Choosing and Booking:

- Book in Advance: Booking well in advance is highly recommended, especially during peak season and for popular treatments.
- Check Online Reviews: Read online reviews from previous clients to get an idea of the spa's quality and services.
- Consider Location and Accessibility: Choose a spa that is conveniently located for you and easily accessible by public transport or taxi.
- Inquire About Packages and Promotions: Many spas offer packages and special offers that can provide good value.
- Communicate Your Needs: When booking, inform the spa of any specific health concerns, allergies, or preferences.

By exploring Malta's diverse spa and wellness scene, you can enhance your vacation with moments of pure relaxation and rejuvenation, returning home feeling refreshed and revitalized.

Day Trip Options

Malta's central location in the Mediterranean makes it an excellent base for exploring the surrounding islands and experiencing the region's diverse offerings. Several captivating day trips are easily accessible from Malta, each offering unique experiences and attractions. This guide explores four exciting day-trip options, providing comprehensive information to help you plan your adventures.

1. Gozo: A Tranquil Escape:

Gozo, Malta's sister island, offers a more rural and tranquil experience compared to the mainland. With its rolling hills, picturesque villages, and stunning coastline, Gozo is a haven for nature lovers and those seeking a peaceful escape.

- Highlights:
    - Victoria (Rabat): Gozo's capital city, with its imposing Citadella offering panoramic views.
    - Ggantija Temples: Megalithic temples dating back to the Neolithic period, among the oldest free-standing structures in the world.
    - Dwejra Bay: A dramatic coastal landscape with the Inland Sea and the Blue Hole (a popular diving spot).
    - Ramla Bay: Gozo's largest sandy beach, known for its reddish-orange sand.
    - Salt Pans: Unique coastal formations used for traditional salt harvesting.
    - Activities: Exploring historical sites, hiking, swimming, diving, relaxing on beaches, enjoying local cuisine.

- Travel Logistics:
    - Ferry: The most common way to reach Gozo is by ferry from Ċirkewwa on Malta's northern coast. The ferry journey takes approximately 25 minutes. There is also a fast ferry service from Valletta to Gozo.
    - Transportation on Gozo: Buses, taxis, car rentals, and scooters are available on Gozo. Buses are a cost-effective option, while renting a car or scooter offers more flexibility.
- Recommended Itinerary:
    - Morning: Take the ferry to Mġarr (Gozo). Visit the Citadella in Victoria and explore its historic streets and fortifications.
    - Lunch: Enjoy a traditional Gozitan lunch at a restaurant in Victoria or Marsalforn.
    - Afternoon: Visit the Ggantija Temples. Explore Dwejra Bay and the Inland Sea. Relax on Ramla Bay.
    - Evening: Return to Malta by ferry.
- Unique Experiences: Experiencing Gozo's more relaxed pace of life, exploring ancient temples, enjoying stunning coastal scenery.
- Entrance Fees: Ggantija Temples: €10. Citadella Visitors Centre: €5.
- Operating Hours: Vary depending on the attraction. Check official websites for up-to-date information.
- Dining Recommendations: Enjoy traditional Gozitan dishes such as ftira (Gozitan pizza), rabbit stew, and local cheese. Several restaurants in Victoria, Marsalforn, and Xlendi offer delicious local cuisine.

2. Comino and the Blue Lagoon: A Tropical Paradise:

Comino, the smallest inhabited island of the Maltese archipelago, is famous for its stunning Blue Lagoon, with crystal-clear turquoise waters.

- Highlights:
    - Blue Lagoon: A shallow, turquoise lagoon perfect for swimming, snorkeling, and relaxing.
    - Santa Marija Tower: A historic watchtower offering panoramic views.
    - Crystal Lagoon: A quieter lagoon with clear waters, ideal for swimming and snorkeling.
    - Activities: Swimming, snorkeling, sunbathing, hiking, exploring the island's coves and bays.
- Travel Logistics:
    - Ferry: Ferries operate to Comino from Ċirkewwa (Malta) and Mġarr (Gozo).
    - Boat Tours: Many boat tours from Malta and Gozo include a stop at the Blue Lagoon.
- Recommended Itinerary:
    - Morning: Take a ferry or boat tour to Comino. Spend the morning swimming and snorkeling in the Blue Lagoon.
    - Lunch: Enjoy a light lunch from one of the food vendors at the Blue Lagoon or bring your own picnic.
    - Afternoon: Explore the island's hiking trails, visit Santa Marija Tower, or relax at one of the quieter bays.
    - Evening: Return to Malta by ferry or boat tour.
- Unique Experiences: Swimming in the incredibly clear turquoise waters of the Blue Lagoon, exploring a virtually uninhabited island.

- Entrance Fees: No entrance fees to the island itself, but there are fees for sunbeds and umbrellas at the Blue Lagoon.
- Operating Hours: Ferries operate throughout the day during the summer months. Check schedules in advance.
- Dining Recommendations: Limited dining options on Comino. It's advisable to bring your own food and drinks, especially during peak season.

3. Popeye Village Malta: A Nostalgic Trip to Sweethaven

Originally built as a film set for the 1980 musical "Popeye," Popeye Village Malta has been transformed into a charming and family-friendly attraction.

- Highlights:
    - The Film Set: Explore the original wooden buildings used in the movie.
    - Shows and Activities: Enjoy live shows, boat trips, and other activities.
    - Swimming and Sunbathing: A small beach area is available for swimming and sunbathing.
- Activities:
    - Exploring the village: Wander through the colorful buildings and discover the various attractions.
    - Watching shows and participating in activities: Enjoy live performances, boat trips, and other entertainment.
    - Swimming and sunbathing: Relax on the small beach.
- Travel Logistics:
    - Bus: Regular bus services connect Valletta and other parts of Malta to Popeye Village.
    - Car: The village is easily accessible by car with parking available.

- Recommended Itinerary:
    - Daytime: Spend a few hours exploring the village, watching shows, and participating in activities.
    - Combine your visit with a trip to nearby beaches like Mellieħa Bay or Golden Bay.
- Entrance Fees: There is an entrance fee to Popeye Village.
- Operating Hours: Check the operating hours before visiting, as they may vary depending on the season.
- Dining Recommendations: There are a few restaurants and cafes within the village.
- Unique Experience: Popeye Village offers a fun and nostalgic experience for all ages, especially for fans of the Popeye cartoon.

4. Marsaxlokk and St. Peter's Pool: Fishing Village Charm and Natural Beauty:

This day trip combines the charm of a traditional fishing village with a stunning natural swimming spot.

- Highlights:
    - Marsaxlokk Bay: A picturesque harbor with colorful fishing boats (luzzus).
    - Sunday Fish Market (if visiting on a Sunday): A bustling market selling fresh seafood and local produce.
    - St. Peter's Pool: A natural rock pool with clear turquoise waters.
    - Activities: Exploring the harbor, visiting the market (on Sundays), swimming, sunbathing, cliff jumping (at St. Peter's Pool).
- Travel Logistics:
    - Bus: Regular bus services connect Valletta and other parts of Malta to Marsaxlokk.

- o   Boat or Walk to St. Peter's Pool: From Marsaxlokk, you can take a short boat trip or walk for about 30 minutes to reach St. Peter's Pool.
- Recommended Itinerary:
  - o   Morning: Visit the Sunday fish market in Marsaxlokk (if visiting on a Sunday). Explore the harbor and enjoy the local atmosphere.
  - o   Lunch: Enjoy fresh seafood at a restaurant in Marsaxlokk.
  - o   Afternoon: Take a boat trip or walk to St. Peter's Pool and enjoy swimming and sunbathing.
  - o   Evening: Return to your accommodation.
- Unique Experiences: Experiencing a traditional Maltese fishing village, swimming in a natural rock pool.
- Entrance Fees: No entrance fees to Marsaxlokk or St. Peter's Pool.
- Operating Hours: The Sunday market operates in the morning.
- Dining Recommendations: Several restaurants in Marsaxlokk offer fresh seafood.

These diverse day trips offer a fantastic opportunity to explore the Maltese archipelago beyond the main island of Malta. By planning your itinerary and considering the practical information provided, you can create unforgettable memories and experience the unique charm of each destination.

CHAPTER SIX

Entertainment And Nightlife Scene

Best Bars and Pubs in Valletta and St. Julian's

Valletta and St. Julian's offer distinct bar and pub experiences, catering to different moods and preferences. Here's a guide to some of the best spots in each location:

Valletta: History, Culture, and Sophisticated Sips

Valletta's bar scene is characterized by its historical settings, intimate ambiance, and focus on quality drinks and conversation.

- Bridge Bar: This iconic open-air bar is a must-visit for its stunning location on a historic bridge overlooking the Grand Harbour. Enjoy live jazz music on Friday nights and soak in the magical atmosphere.
    - Ambiance: Relaxed, romantic, historic, with stunning harbour views.
    - Specialty: Wide selection of wines and spirits, classic cocktails.
    - Address: St Ursula Street, Valletta.
- Strait Street's Resurgence: Once Valletta's entertainment hub, Strait Street has seen a revival with a mix of bars and restaurants. These venues often retain historical features and offer a more intimate and stylish experience.
    - Tico-Tico: This bar evokes the street's past with its vintage decor and lively atmosphere.
    - The Gut: A popular spot with a lively atmosphere and outdoor seating.

- Ambiance: Historic, stylish, lively.
- Specialty: Cocktails, wine, and a selection of beers.
- **The Pub:** This small, traditional pub gained fame as the last place actor Oliver Reed was seen before his death. It's a popular spot for a quiet drink and a taste of Maltese pub culture.
  - Ambiance: Traditional, cozy, historic.
  - Specialty: Beers, spirits, and a friendly atmosphere.
  - Address: 136 Archbishop Street, Valletta.
- **Yard 32:** Tucked away in a back alley off Strait Street, Yard 32 is a gin lover's paradise. With over 100 different gins, it's the perfect place to discover new flavors and enjoy expertly crafted gin and tonics. They also offer a selection of Spanish tapas.
  - Ambiance: Intimate, stylish, specializing in gin.
  - Specialty: Extensive gin selection, Spanish tapas.
  - Address: 32 Strait Street, Valletta.
- **Kamy Cocktail Bar Valletta:** This cocktail bar is known for its expertly crafted cocktails, using fresh ingredients and creative techniques. The bartenders are passionate about mixology and can create bespoke drinks to suit your taste.
  - Ambiance: Stylish, modern, specializing in cocktails.
  - Specialty: Creative cocktails, using fresh ingredients.
  - Address: 60 Old Bakery Street, Valletta.

St. Julian's: Coastal Views and Lively Vibes

St. Julian's offers a mix of relaxed waterfront bars and more energetic venues, particularly in Paceville.

- **23 Sovereign Bar:** Located in the heart of St. Julian's, this bar offers a stylish setting with a focus on cocktails and a vibrant atmosphere.
  - Ambiance: Stylish, lively, specializing in cocktails.

- o Specialty: Creative cocktails, with a focus on presentation.
  - o Address: 23 St Rita Steps, St. Julian's.
- The Dubliner Irish Pub: A popular Irish pub in St. Julian's, offering a lively atmosphere, live music, and a wide selection of beers and spirits.
  - o Ambiance: Lively, traditional Irish pub.
  - o Specialty: Beers, spirits, live music.
  - o Address: St. Julian's Road, St. Julian's.
- Hugo's Lounge: Located in Paceville, Hugo's Lounge offers a more sophisticated experience compared to the surrounding clubs. It's known for its stylish décor, comfortable seating, and extensive cocktail menu.
  - o Ambiance: Stylish, relaxed, specializing in cocktails.
  - o Specialty: Cocktails, premium spirits.
  - o Address: St. Rita Steps, St. Julian's.

Tips for Bar Hopping:

- Valletta: Start your evening with a drink at Bridge Bar for the sunset views, then explore the bars along Strait Street.
- St. Julian's: Head to Paceville for a lively night out, or enjoy a more relaxed evening at one of the waterfront bars.
- Transportation: Taxis and ride-hailing services are readily available in both Valletta and St. Julian's.
- Check for Happy Hour Deals: Many bars offer happy hour deals on drinks.
- Dress Code: Dress codes vary depending on the venue. Valletta bars tend to be more casual, while some St. Julian's venues may have a smart casual dress code.

By exploring these bars and pubs, you can experience the diverse nightlife that Valletta and St. Julian's have to offer, from historical settings and sophisticated cocktails to lively pubs and stunning sea views.

Nightclubs and Late-Night Entertainment

When the sun sets, Malta's energy shifts, and the island comes alive with a vibrant nightlife scene. From high-energy clubs in Paceville to more intimate venues in Valletta, there's something for every taste. This guide focuses on nightclubs and late-night entertainment, providing insights into the hottest spots to dance the night away.

Paceville: Malta's Party Central:

Paceville, located in St. Julian's, remains the undisputed hub for clubbing in Malta. This compact district is packed with clubs, bars, and pubs, offering a diverse range of music and atmospheres.

- Ambiance: Energetic, loud, and crowded, especially on weekends and during the summer months. Expect a party atmosphere with flashing lights, loud music, and packed dance floors.
- Music Genres: Predominantly commercial dance music, house, techno, R&B, hip-hop, and chart hits. Many clubs have multiple rooms with different music genres.
- Key Hotspots (Examples - it's always best to check current listings as clubs change):
- Havana Club: A Paceville institution, Havana is known for its large dance floor, multiple bars, and themed nights. Expect a mix of commercial hits, R&B, and hip-hop.
- Sky Club: One of Malta's largest clubs, Sky Club is known for hosting international DJs and large-scale events, particularly during the summer months. It has a large open-air area and offers stunning views.

- Uno Malta: Located just outside Paceville (but still easily accessible), Uno is a massive open-air club that hosts some of the biggest parties on the island, often featuring internationally renowned DJs. It's particularly popular during the summer months.
- Operating Hours: Clubs in Paceville generally open around 10-11 pm and stay open until the early hours of the morning (3-4 am or later), especially on weekends.
- Special Events: Themed parties, guest DJs, and special events are frequent, especially during peak season (summer). Check local listings or club websites for event schedules.

Tips for Paceville:

- Paceville can be very crowded and noisy, especially on weekends.
- Be prepared for queues to enter popular clubs.
- Drink prices can be higher in Paceville clubs compared to other areas.
- Be aware of your surroundings and take precautions to protect your belongings.

Beyond Paceville: Alternative Late-Night Options:

While Paceville is the main hub, other areas offer alternative late-night entertainment options:

- Gianpula Village (Near Rabat): While not strictly in a town or city center, Gianpula Village is a large complex with multiple clubs and outdoor areas, hosting large-scale events and parties, particularly during the summer. It's known for its open-air setting and diverse music offerings.
- Valletta: While Valletta's nightlife scene is generally more focused on bars and restaurants, some venues stay open later,

offering a more intimate clubbing experience compared to Paceville. Check local listings for specific events and venues.

General Tips for Malta's Nightlife:

- Dress Code: Dress codes vary depending on the venue. Paceville clubs are generally more casual, but some may have stricter dress codes, especially for special events. It's always best to check with the specific venue if you're unsure.
- Entry Fees: Some clubs, especially in Paceville and Gianpula Village, may charge an entrance fee, particularly on weekends or for events with guest DJs.
- Transportation: Taxis and ride-hailing services (Bolt, eCabs) are readily available, especially in Paceville and St. Julian's. Night buses also operate, but service may be limited. Plan your transportation in advance, especially if you're planning a late night out.
- Age Restrictions: The legal drinking age in Malta is 17. Most clubs enforce age restrictions and may require ID.
- Safety: Be aware of your surroundings, especially in crowded areas. Drink responsibly and look after your belongings.

By exploring these nightclubs and late-night entertainment options, you can experience the energetic side of Malta and dance the night away. Remember to check local listings for current events and venue information, as the nightlife scene can evolve.

Cultural Shows and Theatre

Malta's cultural scene is rich and diverse, offering a range of performances that showcase the island's history, traditions, and artistic talent. From grand theatrical productions in historic venues to intimate musical performances and traditional folklore shows, there are plenty of opportunities to immerse yourself in Maltese culture.

Teatru Manoel: A Historic Gem:

Teatru Manoel, located in Valletta, is one of Europe's oldest working theatres. Built in 1731 by Grand Master António Manoel de Vilhena, this stunning theatre is a masterpiece of Baroque architecture.

- Performances: Teatru Manoel hosts a diverse program of performances throughout the year, including opera, ballet, classical music concerts, theatre productions, and more.
- Ambiance: The theatre's ornate interior, with its gilded boxes and painted ceiling, creates a truly magical atmosphere.
- Address: Old Theatre Street, Valletta.
- Tips: Check the theatre's website for the latest schedule of performances and book tickets in advance, especially for popular shows.

Mediterranean Conference Centre: A Grand Setting:

The Mediterranean Conference Centre (MCC), also located in Valletta, is a historic building that hosts a variety of cultural events, including concerts, conferences, and exhibitions.

- Performances: The MCC hosts a range of performances, from classical music concerts to contemporary dance shows.
- Ambiance: The building's grand halls and historic setting create a unique and impressive atmosphere.
- Address: Republic Street, Valletta.
- Tips: Check the MCC's website for upcoming events and performances.

Other Theatres and Performance Spaces:

- Spazju Kreattiv: Located at St James Cavalier in Valletta, Spazju Kreattiv is a contemporary arts center that hosts a variety of performances, exhibitions, and workshops.

- Blue Box Theatre: Located in Msida, the Blue Box Theatre is a smaller venue that hosts theatre productions, music performances, and other cultural events.

Traditional Maltese Folklore Shows:

For a taste of Maltese culture, consider attending a traditional folklore show. These shows typically feature:

- Traditional Music and Dance: Performances of Maltese folk music and dance, often featuring colorful costumes and lively rhythms.
- Local Food and Drinks: Some shows include a traditional Maltese meal or offer local snacks and drinks.
- Locations: Folklore shows are often held in restaurants, hotels, or dedicated performance spaces.
- Tips: Check with your hotel or local tourist information for recommendations and bookings.

Open-Air Performances and Festivals:

During the summer months, Malta hosts various open-air performances and festivals, offering a unique cultural experience.

- Malta Arts Festival: A multi-arts festival that takes place in various locations across Malta, featuring music, theatre, dance, and visual arts.
- Notte Bianca: An annual one-night festival in Valletta that celebrates arts and culture, with museums, galleries, and other cultural venues staying open late and hosting special events.
- Village Festas: Each village in Malta celebrates its patron saint with a festa, a traditional village feast that includes processions, music, fireworks, and other festivities.

Tips for Enjoying Malta's Cultural Shows and Theatre:

- Check Local Listings: Check local newspapers, websites (such as What's On Malta), and tourist information for schedules of performances and events.
- Book Tickets in Advance: For popular shows and events, it's advisable to book tickets in advance.
- Dress Code: Dress codes vary depending on the venue and performance. For formal events at Teatru Manoel or the MCC, smart attire is recommended. For more casual performances or folklore shows, casual attire is acceptable.
- Transportation: Valletta is easily accessible by bus from all over Malta. Taxis and ride-hailing services are also available.

By attending cultural shows and theatre performances in Malta, you can gain a deeper appreciation for the island's rich history, traditions, and artistic talent. Whether you're interested in classical music, theatre, dance, or traditional folklore, you'll find a variety of options to enrich your Maltese experience.

Live Music Venues

Malta's music scene is alive and kicking, offering a diverse range of live music venues that cater to various genres and tastes. From intimate gigs in cozy pubs to energetic performances in larger venues, there's something for every music lover.

Valletta: Intimate Settings and Diverse Genres:

Valletta offers a more intimate and diverse live music scene compared to the larger clubs in Paceville.

- Bridge Bar: As mentioned before, Bridge Bar is not only a great spot for drinks but also a renowned live music venue, particularly for jazz. Enjoy live jazz performances on Friday

evenings in a unique outdoor setting overlooking the Grand Harbour.
- Genre: Jazz.
- Ambiance: Relaxed, atmospheric, outdoor.
- Address: St Ursula Street, Valletta.
- La Bottega: Located on Merchant Street, La Bottega is a popular spot for happy hour and also hosts live music performances, ranging from rock bands to DJs.
- Genre: Varies, including rock, pop, and electronic music.
- Ambiance: Lively, casual.
- Address: Merchant Street, Valletta.
- Strait Street venues: Many bars and restaurants along Strait Street also host live music, often with a focus on blues, jazz, and acoustic sets. Explore the various venues to discover different styles of music.

Beyond Valletta: Diverse Music Experiences:

- Storeroom (Ta' Xbiex): Located just outside Valletta in Ta' Xbiex, Storeroom is a dedicated live music venue that has become a go-to destination for the island's hip and trendy crowd. It showcases a variety of genres, including indie, alternative, electronic, and experimental music.
  o Genre: Indie, alternative, electronic, experimental.
  o Ambiance: Intimate, trendy.
  o Address: Ta' Xbiex.
- The Garage (Żebbuġ): Located in Żebbuġ, The Garage is a popular spot for local rock bands and other live music performances. It has a laid-back atmosphere and is a great place to discover local talent.
  o Genre: Rock, alternative.
  o Ambiance: Laid-back, local.

- o   Address: Żebbuġ.
- The Thirsty Barber (St. Julian's): While primarily known as a cocktail bar, The Thirsty Barber in St. Julian's also hosts live music performances, often featuring local rock bands.
  - o   Genre: Rock, blues.
  - o   Ambiance: Stylish, lively.
  - o   Address: St. Julian's.
- Festivals and Events: Malta hosts several music festivals and events throughout the year, featuring both local and international artists. Check local listings for upcoming events.

Tips for Enjoying Live Music in Malta:

- Check Local Listings: Check local newspapers, websites (such as What's On Malta), and social media for schedules of live music performances.
- Book Tickets in Advance: For popular shows or events, it's advisable to book tickets in advance.
- Arrive Early: For smaller venues, arriving early can help you secure a good spot.
- Support Local Musicians: Many talented local musicians perform in Malta's live music venues. Take the opportunity to discover new music and support the local scene.
- Enjoy the Atmosphere: Malta's live music venues offer a variety of atmospheres, from intimate and relaxed to energetic and lively. Choose a venue that suits your preferences and enjoy the music.

By exploring these live music venues, you can experience the diverse and vibrant music scene that Malta has to offer. Whether you're a fan of jazz, rock, indie, or electronic music, you'll find a venue to suit your taste and enjoy a memorable night out.

CHAPTER SEVEN

CULINARY DELIGHTS

Traditional Maltese Foods: Pastizzi, Rabbit Stew, and More

Maltese cuisine is a delightful blend of Mediterranean influences, with hints of Italian, Sicilian, North African, and British traditions. This unique fusion has resulted in a rich and flavorful culinary heritage, offering a variety of dishes to tantalize your taste buds. Here are some must-try traditional Maltese foods:

Savory Delights:

- Pastizzi: These diamond-shaped flaky pastries are a staple of Maltese cuisine and a popular snack. They are typically filled with ricotta cheese (pastizzi tal-irkotta) or mushy peas (pastizzi tal-piżelli). You'll find pastizzi shops all over Malta, and they're a perfect on-the-go snack or light meal.
- Fenek (Rabbit): Rabbit is considered the national dish of Malta and is prepared in various ways.
    - Stuffat tal-Fenek (Rabbit Stew): This hearty stew is a classic Maltese dish, featuring rabbit braised in a rich tomato and red wine sauce with vegetables such as potatoes, carrots, and onions.
    - Fenek Moqli (Fried Rabbit): Another popular way to enjoy rabbit is by frying it with garlic and herbs.
    - Spaghetti Rabbit Sauce: A flavourful pasta dish with a rich rabbit-based sauce.

- Stuffat tal-Qarnit (Octopus Stew): This flavorful stew features octopus braised in a tomato-based sauce with onions, garlic, and herbs. It's often served with potatoes or pasta.
- Bragioli (Beef Olives): Thin slices of beef rolled and stuffed with a mixture of minced meat, bacon, egg, and herbs, then braised in a rich tomato sauce.
- Timpana: A baked pasta dish similar to a pasta pie, made with macaroni, minced meat, tomato sauce, and cheese.
- Ħobż biż-Żejt (Bread with Oil): A simple but delicious snack or light meal, consisting of a thick slice of Maltese bread rubbed with ripe tomatoes, drizzled with olive oil, and topped with ingredients like tuna, capers, onions, and olives.
- Bigilla: A traditional Maltese dip made from broad beans, garlic, herbs, and chili. It's often served with Maltese bread or crackers.
- Aljotta (Fish Soup): A flavorful fish soup with tomatoes, garlic, herbs, and rice.

Sweet Treats:

- Imqaret: These deep-fried diamond-shaped pastries are filled with a sweet date filling. They are a popular street food and a must-try for those with a sweet tooth.
- Kannoli: Crispy pastry tubes filled with sweet ricotta cheese and often decorated with candied fruit or chocolate chips.
- Qagħaq tal-Għasel (Honey Rings): Ring-shaped biscuits glazed with honey. They are traditionally eaten during Christmas time but are available year-round.
- Figolli: Almond-filled pastries traditionally eaten during Easter. They come in various shapes and are decorated with colorful icing.

Where to Try Traditional Maltese Food:

- Restaurants: Many restaurants throughout Malta specialize in traditional Maltese cuisine. Look for restaurants that are popular with locals for a more authentic experience.
- Pastizzerias: These small shops specialize in pastizzi and other savory pastries. They are a great place to grab a quick and affordable snack.
- Markets: Local markets, such as the Marsaxlokk Sunday fish market, offer opportunities to try local produce and street food.

Tips for Enjoying Maltese Food:

- Be adventurous: Don't be afraid to try new dishes and flavors.
- Ask for recommendations: Locals and restaurant staff can offer valuable recommendations on traditional dishes and local specialties.
- Enjoy the local atmosphere: Maltese restaurants often have a relaxed and welcoming atmosphere. Take your time to savor your meal and enjoy the company.

Maltese cuisine is a delicious reflection of the island's rich history and cultural influences. By trying these traditional dishes, you can gain a deeper understanding of Maltese culture and create a memorable culinary experience.

Best Restaurants and Cafés

Malta's culinary scene is a vibrant reflection of its diverse history and Mediterranean location. From traditional Maltese cuisine to international flavors and innovative dining concepts, there's something to satisfy every palate. This guide highlights some of the best restaurants and cafés across the islands, offering a culinary journey for discerning travelers.

Fine Dining & Special Occasions:

1. ION – The Harbour (Valletta): Located within the Iniala Harbour House, ION boasts Michelin-starred dining with breathtaking views of the Grand Harbour. Chef Alex Dilling creates innovative tasting menus that showcase seasonal ingredients and modern culinary techniques.

- Cuisine: Modern European, Fine Dining.
- Ambiance: Elegant, sophisticated, with panoramic views.
- Address: Iniala Harbour House, 11 St Barbara Bastion, Valletta.
- Hours: Dinner only.
- Reservations: Essential, well in advance.
- Price Range: High-end.

2. de Mondion Restaurant (Mdina): Situated within The Xara Palace Relais & Chateaux, de Mondion offers fine dining with panoramic views from Mdina's bastions. The menu features modern European cuisine with a focus on fresh, seasonal ingredients.

- Cuisine: Modern European, Fine Dining.
- Ambiance: Romantic, elegant, with panoramic views.
- Address: The Xara Palace Relais & Chateaux, Mdina.
- Hours: Lunch and dinner.
- Reservations: Highly recommended.
- Price Range: High-end.

3. Under Grain (Valletta): Another Michelin-starred gem in Valletta, Under Grain offers a unique "farm-to-table" experience. The restaurant focuses on using fresh, locally sourced ingredients and presents them in creative and visually stunning dishes.

- Cuisine: Modern Maltese, Farm-to-Table.
- Ambiance: Stylish, intimate, with a focus on local produce.
- Address: 64 Merchants Street, Valletta.
- Hours: Lunch and dinner.
- Reservations: Highly recommended.
- Price Range: High-end.

Traditional Maltese Cuisine:

1. Legligin (Valletta): This popular restaurant offers a unique dining experience focused on traditional Maltese cuisine. They offer a set tasting menu that showcases a variety of local dishes and flavors.

- Cuisine: Traditional Maltese.
- Ambiance: Cozy, rustic, authentic.
- Address: 117 St Lucia Street, Valletta.
- Hours: Dinner only.
- Reservations: Recommended.
- Price Range: Mid-range.

2. Ta' Marija Restaurant (Mosta): A family-run restaurant that has been serving traditional Maltese cuisine for decades. They offer a wide range of local dishes, including rabbit stew, bragioli, and timpana. They also host folklore shows on certain evenings.

- Cuisine: Traditional Maltese.
- Ambiance: Rustic, family-friendly, traditional.
- Address: Constitution Street, Mosta.
- Hours: Lunch and dinner.
- Reservations: Recommended, especially for folklore shows.
- Price Range: Mid-range.

3. Nenu the Artisan Baker (Valletta): This restaurant specializes in ftira, a traditional Maltese flatbread. They offer a variety of ftira toppings, as well as other traditional Maltese dishes.

- Cuisine: Traditional Maltese, Ftira.
- Ambiance: Casual, rustic, traditional.
- Address: 143 St Dominic Street, Valletta.
- Hours: Lunch and dinner.
- Reservations: Recommended.
- Price Range: Affordable to Mid-range.

Casual Dining & International Flavors:

1. Crust Bistro & Bar (Valletta & St. Julian's): This trendy bistro offers a creative menu with a focus on fresh, locally sourced ingredients. They offer a variety of dishes, from burgers and salads to pasta and seafood.

- Cuisine: Modern European, Bistro.
- Ambiance: Stylish, relaxed, contemporary.
- Addresses: 64 Mensija Street, St. Julian's / 67 Old Bakery Street, Valletta
- Hours: Lunch and dinner.
- Reservations: Recommended, especially during peak hours.
- Price Range: Mid-range.

2. Bocconcino Caffe and restaurant (Sliema): This popular Italian restaurant offers a wide range of pasta dishes, pizzas, and other Italian specialties. They also offer a selection of wines and desserts.

- Cuisine: Italian.
- Ambiance: Cozy, casual, family-friendly.
- Address: 129 Tower Road, Sliema.
- Hours: Breakfast, lunch, and dinner.

- Reservations: Recommended, especially during peak hours.
- Price Range: Mid-range.

3. Zero Sei (Valletta): This popular restaurant serves authentic Roman-style pizza with thin and crispy crusts. They also offer a selection of Italian appetizers and desserts.

- Cuisine: Italian, Pizza.
- Ambiance: Casual, lively.
- Address: 103 Strait Street, Valletta.
- Hours: Lunch and dinner.
- Reservations: Recommended.
- Price Range: Affordable to Mid-range.

Cafés & Light Bites:

1. Fontanella Tea Garden (Mdina): Located within the walls of Mdina, Fontanella Tea Garden offers stunning panoramic views from its rooftop terrace. They are known for their delicious cakes, pastries, and light meals.

- Cuisine: Café, Light Bites.
- Ambiance: Relaxed, scenic, with panoramic views.
- Address: 1 Bastion Street, Mdina.
- Hours: Daytime.
- Reservations: Not usually required.
- Price Range: Affordable.

2. Lot Sixty One Coffee Roasters (Valletta): This specialty coffee shop offers a variety of high-quality coffees, teas, and light snacks. It's a great place to relax and enjoy a good cup of coffee.

- Cuisine: Café, Coffee Shop.
- Ambiance: Modern, minimalist, specializing in coffee.
- Address: 61 Old Bakery Street, Valletta.

- Hours: Daytime.
- Price Range: Affordable.

3. Caffe Cordina (Valletta): A Valletta institution, Caffe Cordina is a grand café located in a historic palazzo. They offer a wide range of coffees, teas, pastries, and light meals.

- Cuisine: Café, Pastry Shop.
- Ambiance: Historic, elegant, traditional.
- Address: 244 Republic Street, Valletta.
- Hours: Daytime.
- Price Range: Affordable to Mid-range.

Tips for Dining in Malta:

- Reservations: It's always a good idea to make reservations, especially for popular restaurants and during peak season.
- Tipping: Tipping is customary in Malta. A 10-15% tip is generally appreciated for good service.
- Local Produce: Many restaurants use fresh, locally sourced ingredients. Look for restaurants that highlight local produce and seafood.
- Maltese Wine: Malta produces its own wine. Try some local wines to complement your meal.
- Dietary Restrictions: Most restaurants can cater to dietary restrictions. It's best to inform them in advance.

By exploring Malta's diverse culinary scene, you can enhance your travel experience and create lasting memories. From fine dining to casual eateries and cozy cafés, there's something to satisfy every culinary craving.

Street Food and Food Market

Malta's street food scene is a vibrant reflection of its diverse culinary influences, offering a delicious and affordable way to experience local flavors. Combined with bustling food markets, it creates a true culinary adventure. Here's a guide to some of the top recommended experiences:

Top Recommended Street Food:

- Pastizzi: These diamond-shaped, flaky pastries are Malta's quintessential street food. Filled with either ricotta cheese (pastizzi tal-irkotta) or mushy peas (pastizzi tal-piżelli), they are a must-try.
    - Highlights: Cheap, readily available, and incredibly satisfying.
    - Where to find them: Pastizzerias are found on almost every street corner. Look for busy ones with locals queuing up – a sign of fresh, tasty pastizzi.
    - Experience: Grab a couple of pastizzi for a quick breakfast or snack on the go.
- Ħobż biż-Żejt (Bread with Oil): This simple yet delicious snack consists of a thick slice of Maltese bread rubbed with ripe tomatoes, drizzled with olive oil, and topped with various ingredients like tuna, capers, onions, and olives.
    - Highlights: Fresh, flavorful, and a great representation of Mediterranean cuisine.
    - Where to find them: Cafés, snack bars, and some street food stalls.
    - Experience: Enjoy it as a light lunch or a snack with a cold drink.
- Imqaret: These deep-fried, diamond-shaped pastries filled with a sweet date filling are a popular sweet treat.

- o Highlights: Sweet, sticky, and satisfying.
- o Where to find them: Street food stalls, markets, and some bakeries.
- o Experience: Perfect for a sweet ending to a meal or as a snack.
- Qubbajt (Nougat): This traditional Maltese nougat is made with honey, almonds, and other nuts.
  - o Highlights: Sweet, chewy, and nutty.
  - o Where to find them: Markets, sweet shops, and some street vendors.
  - o Experience: A popular treat during festas and other celebrations.

Top Recommended Food Markets:

- Marsaxlokk Fish Market (Marsaxlokk): Held every Sunday morning in the picturesque fishing village of Marsaxlokk, this market is a feast for the senses.
  - o Location: Marsaxlokk Bay, Southern Malta.
  - o Highlights: Freshly caught seafood, vibrant atmosphere, colorful luzzus (traditional fishing boats).
  - o Signature Dishes/Experiences: While you won't find cooked street food within the fish market itself (it's primarily raw fish), the surrounding restaurants serve incredibly fresh seafood dishes. Enjoy a meal at a waterfront restaurant after browsing the market.
  - o Tips: Arrive early for the best selection and to avoid crowds.
- Is-Suq tal-Belt (Valletta Food Market): Located in a restored Victorian market hall in Valletta, Is-Suq tal-Belt offers a modern food market experience.
  - o Location: Merchant Street, Valletta.

- o Highlights: Diverse food stalls offering Maltese and international cuisine, sit-down dining options, bars, and a pleasant atmosphere.
- o Signature Dishes/Experiences: Try traditional Maltese dishes like rabbit stew or horse meat stew at some of the stalls. Enjoy a craft beer or local wine at one of the bars.
- o Tips: A great place for lunch or dinner, especially if you're traveling with a group with diverse tastes.

Street Food Safety Tips:

- Look for Cleanliness: Choose stalls and vendors that appear clean and hygienic. Check if the vendor is wearing gloves and if the food is stored properly.
- Freshly Cooked Food: Opt for food that is cooked fresh in front of you. Avoid food that has been sitting out for a long time.
- Hot Food Should Be Hot: Ensure that hot food is served piping hot.
- Check for Crowds: Popular stalls with long queues are often a good sign of quality and freshness, as it indicates high turnover of food.
- Use Your Senses: Trust your instincts. If something looks or smells suspicious, avoid it.
- Stay Hydrated: Drink plenty of bottled water, especially during hot weather.
- Be Mindful of Allergies: If you have any food allergies, be sure to ask the vendor about the ingredients.

By following these tips and exploring Malta's street food and food markets, you can enjoy a delicious and safe culinary adventure, experiencing the authentic flavors of the island.

Wine and Local Spirits: Maltese Wines and Kinnie

While Malta might not be as internationally renowned for its wine as some of its European neighbors, the islands have a long history of winemaking, dating back to the Roman era. In recent years, Maltese winemakers have been producing increasingly high-quality wines, utilizing both international and indigenous grape varieties. Alongside wine, Malta also boasts a unique local soft drink called Kinnie, which has become a national favorite.

Maltese Wines: A Growing Reputation:

Malta's warm Mediterranean climate and unique terroir provide ideal conditions for growing grapes. While the islands are small, they produce a surprising variety of wines, including reds, whites, and rosés.

- Indigenous Grape Varieties:
    - Ġellewża: This red grape variety is unique to Malta and produces light to medium-bodied wines with fruity and spicy notes.
    - Girgentina: This white grape variety is also indigenous to Malta and produces crisp, dry wines with citrus and floral aromas.
- International Grape Varieties: Maltese winemakers also cultivate international grape varieties such as Cabernet Sauvignon, Merlot, Syrah, Chardonnay, and Sauvignon Blanc.

Notable Wineries:

- Marsovin: One of Malta's oldest and largest wineries, producing a wide range of wines, including their renowned Grand Maître and Antonin Blanc.

- Delicata: Another long-established winery known for its Classic Collection and Medina range.
- Meridiana Wine Estate: A boutique winery known for its premium wines, including Isis (Chardonnay) and Nexus (Merlot).

Where to Taste Maltese Wine:

- Wine Bars: Many wine bars in Valletta and other towns offer a selection of Maltese wines by the glass or bottle.
- Restaurants: Most restaurants in Malta offer a selection of local wines on their wine lists.
- Winery Tours: Some wineries, such as Meridiana, offer tours and tastings.

Kinnie: Malta's Unique Soft Drink:

Kinnie is a unique non-alcoholic beverage that has become a national favorite in Malta. It's a bittersweet carbonated drink made from chinotto oranges and aromatic herbs.

- Taste: Kinnie has a distinctive bittersweet flavor with hints of citrus and herbs. It's often described as an acquired taste, but many visitors quickly become fans.
- Where to Find Kinnie: Kinnie is widely available throughout Malta in supermarkets, restaurants, bars, and cafes.
- Kinnie Spritz: A popular way to enjoy Kinnie is as a spritz, mixed with white wine or Prosecco.
- Variations: There are also diet and sugar-free versions of Kinnie available.

Other Local Spirits:

While wine and Kinnie are the most well-known beverages in Malta, there are also some local spirits worth trying:

- Bajtra (Prickly Pear Liqueur): A sweet liqueur made from prickly pears, a fruit that grows abundantly in Malta.
- Limoncello: A lemon liqueur that is popular throughout Italy and also produced in Malta.

Tips for Enjoying Maltese Wine and Local Spirits:

- Try the local varieties: Don't miss the opportunity to try wines made from the indigenous Ġellewża and Girgentina grapes.
- Pair with local food: Maltese wines pair well with traditional Maltese cuisine.
- Enjoy Kinnie as a refreshing drink: Kinnie is a perfect thirst quencher on a hot day.
- Visit a winery: If you have time, consider visiting a local winery for a tour and tasting.
- Enjoy responsibly: Drink alcohol in moderation and be aware of your limits.

By exploring Malta's wine and local spirits, you can discover another aspect of the island's rich culture and enjoy unique flavors that are specific to the Maltese archipelago.

Where to Find the Best Seafood

Malta, surrounded by the bountiful Mediterranean Sea, is a seafood lover's paradise. Fresh catches are brought in daily, and many restaurants specialize in preparing them in traditional Maltese and Mediterranean styles. Here's a guide to finding the best seafood on the islands:

1. Marsaxlokk: The Fishing Village Hub:

Marsaxlokk, a picturesque fishing village in the south of Malta, is arguably the best place to find fresh seafood. The daily catch is brought directly to the harbor, and many restaurants line the waterfront, offering stunning views and the freshest possible seafood.

- Why Marsaxlokk? The village's economy is centered around fishing, ensuring a constant supply of fresh seafood. The Sunday fish market is a must-visit for experiencing the local fishing culture and seeing the variety of catches.
- Restaurants to try:
  - Tartarun Restaurant: Known for its refined seafood dishes and elegant setting.
  - Roots Restaurant: Offers a more casual dining experience with a focus on fresh, seasonal seafood.
  - Many other family-run restaurants line the harbor, offering delicious and affordable seafood dishes.
- Tips for Marsaxlokk: Visit on a Sunday to experience the bustling fish market. Arrive early for lunch to secure a table at a popular restaurant.

2. Valletta: Seafood with a View:

Valletta, Malta's capital city, also offers excellent seafood dining options, often with stunning views of the Grand Harbour.

- Why Valletta? Many restaurants in Valletta focus on using fresh, local ingredients, including seafood. The city's historic setting and beautiful views enhance the dining experience.
- Restaurants to try:
  - Porticello Restaurant: Located on the waterfront, Porticello offers stunning views of Valletta and a menu featuring fresh seafood and Mediterranean dishes.
  - The Oyster Grotto: Specializes in fresh oysters and other seafood delicacies.

- Other restaurants along the Valletta Waterfront: Offer a variety of seafood options with beautiful harbour views.

3. Coastal Towns and Villages:

Many coastal towns and villages around Malta and Gozo offer excellent seafood restaurants.

- Gozo:
    - Xlendi Bay: This picturesque bay in Gozo is home to several restaurants offering fresh seafood with beautiful sea views.
    - Marsalforn: Another popular coastal town in Gozo with a variety of seafood restaurants.
- Other locations:
    - Mellieħa: Several restaurants in Mellieħa offer fresh seafood with views of Mellieħa Bay.
    - St. Julian's and Sliema: These popular tourist areas also offer a variety of seafood restaurants, although they may be more tourist-oriented.

Tips for Choosing a Seafood Restaurant:

- Look for daily specials: Many restaurants offer daily specials based on the fresh catch of the day.
- Ask about the origin of the seafood: Inquire about where the seafood is sourced to ensure freshness.
- Consider the setting: Choose a restaurant with a view of the sea for a more immersive experience.
- Check online reviews: Read reviews from other diners to get an idea of the restaurant's quality and service.

Must-Try Seafood Dishes:

- Lampuki Pie: A traditional Maltese pie filled with lampuki fish (a seasonal fish that arrives in late summer/autumn).

- Aljotta: A traditional Maltese fish soup.
- Grilled fish: Freshly grilled fish, such as sea bass, sea bream, or swordfish.
- Octopus stew: A flavorful stew with octopus, tomatoes, and onions.

By exploring these locations and trying the local specialties, you can experience the best seafood that Malta has to offer.

Foodie Travel Tips

Malta's culinary scene is a vibrant mix of tradition and innovation, offering a delightful experience for food lovers. To make the most of your culinary journey, consider these practical tips for navigating the local dining landscape:

Reservations: Plan Ahead, Especially During Peak Season:

- Fine Dining and Popular Restaurants: Reservations are highly recommended, especially for fine dining establishments, popular restaurants, and during peak tourist season (summer months, holidays, and weekends). Booking in advance ensures you secure a table and avoid disappointment. Online booking platforms or direct phone calls to the restaurant are common methods.
- Smaller Eateries and Cafés: While reservations may not always be necessary for smaller eateries and cafés, it's still a good idea to check, particularly if you're dining during peak hours or with a larger group.
- Special Events and Festas: During village festas (traditional village feasts) and other special events, restaurants can be extremely busy. Booking well in advance is essential.

Peak Dining Hours: Timing is Key:

- Lunch: Lunch in Malta is typically served between 12:30 pm and 2:30 pm. Arriving during this period ensures you have the full menu available.
- Dinner: Dinner service usually starts around 7:00 pm and can continue until late. Peak dinner hours are generally between 8:00 pm and 10:00 pm. Arriving slightly earlier or later might help you avoid the biggest crowds.
- Local Habits: Locals often dine later than in some other European countries, especially during the summer.

Trying New Things: Embrace the Local Flavors:

- Be Adventurous: Don't be afraid to step outside your comfort zone and try traditional Maltese dishes. Ask locals or restaurant staff for recommendations. Some must-tries include rabbit stew (stuffat tal-fenek), lampuki pie (seasonal fish pie), bragioli (beef olives), and ftira (Maltese flatbread).
- Visit Local Markets: Exploring local markets, such as the Marsaxlokk fish market or the Ta' Qali farmers' market, provides an excellent opportunity to discover fresh local produce and sample street food.
- Pastizzerias: These small shops specializing in pastizzi (flaky pastries filled with ricotta or peas) are a great place for a quick, affordable, and authentic Maltese snack.
- Local Wines: Malta produces its own wines, often from indigenous grape varieties like Ġellewża (red) and Girgentina (white). Don't hesitate to ask for recommendations or try a local wine with your meal.
- Kinnie: This unique bittersweet soft drink made from chinotto oranges and herbs is a local favorite. It's an acquired taste but worth trying for a truly Maltese experience.

- Ask for Recommendations: Locals are usually happy to share their favorite restaurants and dishes. Don't hesitate to ask your hotel staff, tour guides, or even fellow diners for recommendations.
- Food Festivals and Events: Check local event listings for food festivals and events, which offer a great opportunity to sample a variety of Maltese cuisine in one place.

By following these practical tips, you can navigate Malta's culinary scene with confidence, discover hidden gems, and enjoy a truly memorable dining experience.

CHAPTER EIGHT

Shopping in Malta

Modern Shopping Centers

Beyond its historic streets and traditional markets, Malta offers modern shopping centers that provide a contemporary retail experience, combining diverse shopping options with dining, entertainment, and leisure. These malls cater to both locals and tourists seeking convenience and variety.

1. The Point Shopping Mall (Sliema): Premier Waterfront Destination:

Located at Tigné Point in Sliema, The Point is Malta's largest shopping mall, offering stunning views of Valletta across the harbor. Its modern architecture and spacious layout create a relaxed and stylish shopping environment.

- Retail Offerings: The Point boasts a wide selection of international fashion brands (e.g., Mango, Tommy Hilfiger, Guess, United Colors of Benetton), popular high-street retailers, perfumeries, jewelry stores, bookstores (Agenda Bookshop), and a large Marks & Spencer department store offering clothing, homeware, and food.
- Dining Options: A diverse food court and various restaurants/cafés provide options for quick bites, casual meals, and more formal dining. Many offer outdoor seating with scenic sea views.
- Entertainment and Amenities: A large Pavi Supermarket caters to grocery needs. The open-air piazza frequently hosts seasonal events, exhibitions, and performances, creating a

vibrant atmosphere. Restrooms, baby changing facilities, and ATMs are readily available.
- Location/Address: Tigné Point, Sliema, Malta.
- Hours of Operation: Generally 10:00 am to 9:00 pm daily. Individual store and restaurant hours may vary.
- Parking: Ample underground parking is available with direct access to the mall via elevators and escalators. Parking fees apply.
- Special Events/Promotions: The Point regularly hosts seasonal sales, fashion shows, promotional events, and festive activities. Check their official website or social media pages for the latest updates and event schedules.

2. Bay Street Shopping Complex (St. Julian's): Entertainment and Retail Hub:

Located in the heart of St. Julian's, Bay Street offers a different kind of shopping experience, blending retail with entertainment and leisure activities in an open-air setting.

- Retail Offerings: Bay Street features a mix of fashion boutiques, souvenir shops, jewelry stores, and specialized retailers catering to tourists and locals. While it may not have the same concentration of high-end international brands as The Point, it offers a more varied selection of smaller shops and unique finds.
- Dining Options: A variety of restaurants, cafés, and bars are situated throughout the complex, offering diverse culinary options, from casual dining to international cuisine. Many establishments offer outdoor seating overlooking St. George's Bay.
- Entertainment and Amenities: Bay Street is known for its entertainment offerings, including a multi-screen cinema

(Eden Cinemas), a bowling alley (Eden SuperBowl), and a casino (Casino Malta). The central courtyard frequently hosts live music performances, events, and family-friendly activities, creating a lively atmosphere.

- Location/Address: St. George's Bay, St. Julian's, Malta.
- Hours of Operation: Shops generally operate from 10:00 am to 10:00 pm daily. Entertainment venues and some restaurants may stay open later.
- Parking: Underground parking is available.
- Special Events/Promotions: Bay Street is known for its regular events, including live music, themed parties, seasonal promotions, and family-oriented activities. Check their website or social media for current listings.

3. Embassy Shopping Complex (Valletta): Convenient City Center Shopping:

Located on Strait Street in Valletta, Embassy Shopping Complex offers a more compact but convenient shopping experience within the capital city.

- Retail Offerings: A selection of fashion stores, beauty shops, a supermarket (Valletta Supermarket), and other retailers catering to everyday needs.
- Dining Options: A food court and cafés provide casual dining options.
- Entertainment and Amenities: A multi-screen cinema (Embassy Cinemas) is a key attraction.
- Location/Address: Strait Street, Valletta, Malta.
- Hours of Operation: Generally 9:00 am to 7:00 pm (may vary).

- Parking: Limited street parking is available within Valletta. It's recommended to utilize the MCP car park just outside the city walls and enter Valletta on foot or by public transport.
- Special Events/Promotions: Occasional promotions and events are offered.

4. Arkadia Commercial Centre (Victoria, Gozo): Gozo's Modern Shopping Hub:

Located in Victoria, Gozo's capital city, Arkadia provides a modern shopping destination for both Gozo residents and visitors.

- Retail Offerings: A mix of fashion stores, a large supermarket (Arkadi Supermarket), household goods, and other retailers.
- Dining Options: Cafés and a restaurant.
- Entertainment and Amenities: A multi-screen cinema is located nearby.
- Location/Address: Fortunato Mizzi Street, Victoria, Gozo, Malta.
- Hours of Operation: Generally 9:00 am to 7:00 pm (may vary).
- Parking: Parking is available.
- Special Events/Promotions: Occasional promotions and events are offered.

Tips for Shopping at Malta's Modern Shopping Centers:

- Check Opening Hours: Verify specific store and restaurant opening hours, especially on Sundays and public holidays.
- Look for Sales: Take advantage of seasonal sales and promotions.
- Transportation: Consider public transport or parking options, especially within Valletta where parking is limited.

- Combine with Other Activities: The central locations of these malls allow you to easily combine shopping with sightseeing, dining, or other leisure activities.

These modern shopping centers complement Malta's traditional shopping scene, offering convenient and varied retail experiences that cater to a wide range of needs and preferences.

Local Markets and Souvenir Shops

Malta's shopping experience extends far beyond modern malls. The island's local markets and souvenir shops offer a vibrant glimpse into Maltese culture, providing opportunities to discover unique handcrafted goods, local delicacies, and memorable keepsakes. Exploring these bustling hubs is a treasure hunt, allowing you to connect with local artisans and experience the authentic spirit of Malta.

Vibrant Local Markets: A Sensory Feast:

- Marsaxlokk Fish Market (Marsaxlokk): This iconic Sunday market is a must-see. The picturesque fishing village transforms into a bustling marketplace where fishermen sell their fresh catch directly from their colorful luzzus (traditional fishing boats).
    - Location: Marsaxlokk Bay, Southern Malta.
    - When: Every Sunday morning (best visited early).
    - Specialties: Fresh seafood, local produce, honey, jams, and other local products.
    - Cultural Significance: This market is deeply rooted in Maltese fishing tradition and provides a glimpse into the local way of life.
    - Tip: Arrive early to witness the lively atmosphere and secure the freshest seafood.

- Is-Suq tal-Belt (Valletta Food Market): Located in a beautifully restored Victorian market hall in Valletta, Is-Suq tal-Belt offers a modern take on the traditional market experience. It features a variety of food stalls, restaurants, and bars, showcasing Maltese cuisine and international flavors.
    - Location: Merchant Street, Valletta.
    - When: Daily (check individual stall opening times).
    - Specialties: Diverse food offerings, local produce, street food, sit-down meals.
    - Cultural Significance: The market building itself is a historical landmark, and the market provides a contemporary hub for food and social interaction.
    - Tip: A great place for lunch or a snack while exploring Valletta.
- Ta' Qali Crafts Village (Attard): This crafts village is a haven for those seeking authentic Maltese crafts. Artisans work on-site, creating beautiful handmade items, including glass, pottery, lace, silver filigree, and jewelry.
    - Location: Ta' Qali, Attard, Central Malta.
    - When: Daily (individual shop hours vary).
    - Specialties: Maltese glass, pottery, lace, silver filigree, jewelry, and other crafts.
    - Cultural Significance: Ta' Qali is dedicated to preserving and promoting traditional Maltese crafts.
    - Tip: A great place to see craftspeople at work and purchase unique, high-quality souvenirs directly from the source.
- Il-Monti (Valletta Street Market): Held along Merchant Street in Valletta, Il-Monti is a traditional street market offering a variety of goods, including clothing, souvenirs, household items, and sometimes local snacks.
    - Location: Merchant Street, Valletta.

- o When: Daily (mainly mornings).
- o Specialties: Souvenirs, clothing, household goods.
- o Cultural Significance: This market has been a part of Valletta's streetscape for many years.
- o Tip: Be prepared to haggle politely for better prices.

Souvenir Shopping: Memorable Keepsakes:

- Maltese Lace (Bizzilla): Delicate and intricate, Maltese lace is a beautiful and timeless souvenir. Look for doilies, tablecloths, scarves, and other items.
- Maltese Glass: Known for its vibrant colors and unique designs, Maltese glass is a popular choice. Visit glass factories in Mdina or Ta' Qali to see glassblowing demonstrations.
- Maltese Pottery: Characterized by its bold colors and traditional patterns, Maltese pottery makes a practical and decorative souvenir.
- Silver Filigree: Intricate and delicate silverwork is another traditional Maltese craft. Look for jewelry, ornaments, and other decorative items.
- Food Products: Local honey, particularly Gozo honey, is a delicious souvenir. You can also find local jams, preserves, and olive oil.
- Maltese Cross: This eight-pointed cross, a symbol of Malta, is a popular motif found on various souvenirs, from jewelry to keychains.

Tips for Shopping in Malta:

- Bargaining: Polite bargaining is acceptable at some markets and smaller shops, but not in larger stores or established boutiques.

- Authenticity: Look for the "Made in Malta" label to ensure you are purchasing authentic Maltese products.
- Support Local Artisans: Buying directly from artisans supports the local economy and helps preserve traditional crafts.
- Check for Quality: Inspect items carefully before purchasing them.
- Interact with Vendors: Engaging with vendors can enhance your shopping experience and provide insights into Maltese culture.

Exploring Malta's local markets and souvenir shops offers a unique and enriching experience, allowing you to discover the island's rich cultural heritage and find memorable keepsakes to cherish.

Specialty Shops and Boutiques

Beyond the bustling markets and modern malls, Malta hides a treasure trove of specialty shops and boutiques, showcasing the island's rich craftsmanship and unique local products. These hidden gems offer a more personalized shopping experience, allowing you to discover authentic Maltese souvenirs and support local artisans.

Handcrafted Treasures:

1. Maltese Lace (Bizzilla): Bizzilla, the intricate Maltese lace, is a testament to the island's rich heritage. Look for delicate doilies, tablecloths, scarves, and other items crafted with fine threads and traditional patterns.

- Where to Find It:
    - Gozo: The island of Gozo is renowned for its lace-making tradition. Explore villages like Gharb and Xewkija, where you might find local women selling their handmade lace. The

- Koperattiva Ghawdxija tal-Bizzilla u Artigjanat (Gozo Lace Cooperative) is also a good option.
  - Ta' Qali Crafts Village (Attard): Several shops in Ta' Qali offer Maltese lace alongside other crafts.
  - Valletta: Some shops in Valletta, particularly along Merchant Street, also sell lace items.

2. Maltese Silver Filigree: This delicate art form involves creating intricate designs from fine silver threads. Look for jewelry, ornaments, and other decorative items.

- Where to Find It:
  - Ta' Qali Crafts Village (Attard): Ta' Qali is a prime location for finding silver filigree. You can often watch silversmiths at work.
  - Valletta: Jewelry shops along Republic Street and Merchant Street in Valletta also offer a selection of Maltese silver filigree.

3. Maltese Pottery: Characterized by its vibrant colors, traditional patterns, and unique shapes, Maltese pottery makes a beautiful and practical souvenir.

- Where to Find It:
  - Ta' Qali Crafts Village (Attard): Ta' Qali is the main center for Maltese pottery, with numerous workshops and shops offering a wide variety of items.
  - Mdina: Some shops in Mdina also sell Maltese pottery.

4. Handmade Jewelry: Beyond silver filigree, Malta also boasts talented jewelry designers creating unique pieces using various materials, including glass, semi-precious stones, and traditional Maltese motifs.

- Where to Find It:
    - Valletta: Explore the side streets and quieter areas of Valletta for independent jewelry boutiques.
    - Ta' Qali Crafts Village (Attard): Some artisans in Ta' Qali create and sell their own jewelry.

Gourmet Specialties and Local Delicacies:

1. Maltese Honey: Known for its unique flavor derived from the local flora, Maltese honey, especially from Gozo, is a delicious and natural souvenir.

- Where to Find It:
    - Ta' Qali Farmers' Market (Attard): You can often find local honey directly from producers at this market.
    - Specialty Food Shops: Many shops across Malta specialize in local food products, including honey.

2. Local Liqueurs: Malta produces several unique liqueurs, including Bajtra (prickly pear liqueur) and various citrus liqueurs.

- Where to Find It:
    - Specialty Food Shops: Shops specializing in local food and drink products often carry these liqueurs.
    - Duty-Free Shops at the Airport: A convenient option for last-minute purchases.

3. Maltese Wine: While available in most restaurants and supermarkets, visiting a local winery can provide a more immersive experience.

- Where to Find It:
    - Wineries: Some wineries, like Meridiana Wine Estate, offer tours and tastings.

- Wine Shops: Several wine shops in Valletta and other towns offer a wide selection of Maltese wines.

Unique Boutique Experiences:

- Il-Lokal (Valletta): This concept store showcases the work of local designers and artisans, offering a curated selection of clothing, jewelry, homeware, and artwork.
- Souvenirs That Don't Suck (Valletta): This shop offers a refreshing take on traditional souvenirs, focusing on quirky, creative, and well-designed items.

Tips for Shopping at Specialty Shops and Boutiques:

- Take Your Time: These shops offer a more personalized experience. Take your time to browse, ask questions, and learn about the products and the artisans.
- Support Local Businesses: By shopping at these smaller shops, you're directly supporting the local economy and helping to preserve traditional crafts.
- Look for Unique Items: These shops are a great place to find one-of-a-kind souvenirs and gifts.
- Check Opening Hours: Opening hours can vary, especially for smaller shops. It's always a good idea to check before you go.
- Visit Ta' Qali Crafts Village: This is a must if you want to see artisans at work and purchase items directly from them.

By exploring Malta's specialty shops and boutiques, you can discover unique treasures, support local artisans, and bring home truly memorable keepsakes that reflect the island's rich culture and heritage.

Shopping Etiquette and Tips

Navigating Malta's diverse shopping landscape, from bustling markets to quaint boutiques, requires a blend of savvy and cultural sensitivity. Here are some practical tips to enhance your shopping experience:

Bargaining: A Nuance of Negotiation:

- Where Bargaining is Appropriate: Bargaining is generally acceptable in traditional markets like Il-Monti in Valletta and sometimes at smaller stalls in Marsaxlokk. It's less common in established shops, boutiques, and shopping malls.
- The Art of Negotiation: Approach bargaining with a friendly and respectful demeanor. Start with a polite inquiry about the price and then offer a slightly lower price than what you're willing to pay. Be prepared to meet somewhere in the middle. Avoid being overly aggressive or demanding.
- When Not to Bargain: It's generally not appropriate to bargain in department stores, established shops with fixed prices, or when purchasing handcrafted items directly from artisans in their workshops. In these cases, the prices are usually set to reflect the quality and craftsmanship.

Cultural Considerations: Respecting Local Customs:

- Greetings: A simple "hello" or "bonġu" (good morning/good day) is appreciated when entering a shop or approaching a stall.
- Patience: Take your time browsing and avoid rushing vendors. Maltese shopkeepers are generally friendly and helpful.
- Respect for Handicrafts: Show genuine appreciation for the craftsmanship of handmade items. Avoid overly critical comments or attempts to drastically undervalue their work.

- Language: While English is widely spoken in Malta, learning a few basic Maltese phrases can be a nice gesture and may even help with bargaining.
- Sunday Shopping: Many smaller shops and markets have limited hours or are closed on Sundays, particularly in smaller towns and villages. Plan your shopping accordingly.

Reputable Sellers: Ensuring Authenticity and Quality:

- Government-Licensed Shops: Look for shops displaying government licenses or certifications, which indicate adherence to quality standards.
- Direct from Artisans: Purchasing directly from artisans at Ta' Qali Crafts Village or in Gozo's villages ensures authenticity and supports local craftsmanship.
- Established Shops: Well-established shops and boutiques with a long history are generally reliable sources for quality goods.
- Check for "Made in Malta" Labels: When purchasing souvenirs, look for the "Made in Malta" label to ensure the item was produced locally.
- Avoid Suspiciously Low Prices: If a price seems too good to be true, it might be a sign of a counterfeit or low-quality product.
- Ask for Receipts: Always ask for a receipt as proof of purchase, especially for more expensive items.

By following these practical tips, you can navigate Malta's shopping scene with confidence, respect local customs, and find authentic and memorable souvenirs.

CHAPTER NINE

CULTURAL EXPERIENCES

Festivals and Events

Malta's calendar is packed with vibrant festivals and events, offering a glimpse into the island's rich culture, history, and traditions. From religious feasts to music festivals and historical reenactments, there's something to captivate every visitor.

1. Valletta Baroque Festival:

   - When: January (typically two weeks).
   - Where: Various venues in Valletta, primarily Teatru Manoel and St. John's Co-Cathedral.
   - Significance: Celebrates Baroque music and its connection to Valletta's architectural heritage.
   - What to Expect: Performances by renowned international and local musicians, featuring Baroque orchestras, chamber music ensembles, and soloists.
   - Practical Information: Book tickets well in advance, as popular performances sell out quickly. Valletta is easily accessible by public transport. Accommodation options are plentiful in Valletta and nearby Sliema.

2. Carnival (Karnival):

   - When: February (leading up to Ash Wednesday).
   - Where: Valletta is the main hub, with celebrations also taking place in other towns and villages, particularly Nadur in Gozo.
   - Significance: A pre-Lenten celebration with roots in medieval traditions, featuring colorful costumes, floats, parades, and street parties.

- What to Expect: Elaborate floats, costumed participants, street performances, music, dancing, and a general atmosphere of revelry. Nadur's Carnival is known for its more spontaneous and macabre celebrations.
- Practical Information: Valletta can be crowded during Carnival. Book accommodation and transportation in advance. Public transport is available, but expect delays.

3. Holy Week and Easter:

    - When: Holy Week (the week leading up to Easter Sunday).
    - Where: Throughout Malta and Gozo, with processions and religious ceremonies taking place in churches and streets.
    - Significance: The most important religious period in Malta, commemorating the passion, death, and resurrection of Jesus Christ.
    - What to Expect: Solemn processions, church services, and traditional displays. Good Friday processions are particularly moving, featuring participants dressed as biblical figures.
    - Practical Information: Check local church schedules for service times and procession routes. Accommodation should be booked in advance, especially if traveling during Holy Week itself.

4. Malta International Arts Festival:

    - When: Summer (typically June/July).
    - Where: Various venues across Malta, including Valletta, Gozo, and other locations.
    - Significance: A multi-arts festival showcasing a diverse program of music, theatre, dance, and visual arts.

- What to Expect: Performances by international and local artists, ranging from classical music and opera to contemporary dance and theatre.
- Practical Information: Check the festival website for the program and book tickets in advance.

5. Village Festas (Festi):

- When: Throughout the summer months (May to September), with each village celebrating its patron saint on a specific date.
- Where: Each village has its own festa, centered around the local parish church.
- Significance: Celebrations of the village's patron saint, featuring religious processions, band marches, fireworks, and street parties.
- What to Expect: Colorful decorations, band marches through the streets, spectacular fireworks displays, food stalls, and a lively atmosphere.
- Practical Information: Check local calendars or tourist information for festa dates and locations. Each festa is unique, so experiencing a few different ones can be rewarding.

6. Notte Bianca:

- When: Typically in October.
- Where: Valletta.
- Significance: A one-night festival celebrating arts and culture, with museums, galleries, and other cultural venues staying open late and hosting special events.
- What to Expect: Free access to museums and galleries, live music performances, street art installations, theatre performances, and other cultural activities.

- Practical Information: Valletta can be very crowded during Notte Bianca. Public transport is recommended.

General Tips for Attending Maltese Festivals:

- Book Accommodation and Transportation in Advance: Especially during peak season and for popular events.
- Check Local Listings and Websites: For the most up-to-date information on dates, times, and venues.
- Embrace the Local Culture: Participate in the festivities and interact with locals to experience the true spirit of the event.
- Be Prepared for Crowds: Especially during popular events in Valletta.
- Respect Religious Traditions: During religious events like Holy Week and village festas, dress respectfully and be mindful of local customs.

By planning your trip around these festivals and events, you can experience the vibrant heart of Maltese culture and create lasting memories.

Museums and Arts Galleries

Malta's rich history and vibrant culture are beautifully showcased in its diverse museums and art galleries. From ancient artifacts to contemporary masterpieces, these cultural institutions offer a fascinating journey through time and creativity.

Museums: Exploring Malta's Past:

- MUŻA – The National Community Art Museum (Valletta): Housed in the historic Auberge d'Italie, MUŻA showcases a collection of Maltese art from the medieval period to the present day.

- o Highlights: Works by renowned Maltese artists, including Mattia Preti and Antonio Sciortino. The museum also focuses on community engagement and offers interactive exhibits.
  - o Location: Merchants Street, Valletta.
  - o Practical Information: Check their website for opening hours and ticket prices.
- National Museum of Archaeology (Valletta): This museum houses a remarkable collection of prehistoric artifacts, providing insights into Malta's ancient history.
  - o Highlights: The "Sleeping Lady" figurine, a unique example of prehistoric Maltese art.
  - o Location: Republic Street, Valletta.
  - o Practical Information: Check their website for opening hours and ticket prices.
- Fort St. Elmo – National War Museum (Valletta): This historic fort played a crucial role in Malta's history, particularly during the Great Siege of 1565 and World War II. The museum showcases exhibits related to Malta's military history.
  - o Highlights: Exhibits on the Great Siege, World War II, and Malta's role in the Mediterranean.
  - o Location: Valletta.
  - o Practical Information: Check their website for opening hours and ticket prices.
- The Inquisitor's Palace (Birgu): This historic palace offers a fascinating glimpse into the workings of the Roman Inquisition in Malta.
  - o Highlights: The preserved Inquisitor's chambers and the historical exhibits on the Inquisition.
  - o Location: Birgu (Vittoriosa).

- Practical Information: Check their website for opening hours and ticket prices.
- Malta Maritime Museum (Birgu): This museum explores Malta's long maritime history, from ancient seafaring to the Knights of St. John and the British era.
  - Highlights: Exhibits on shipbuilding, navigation, and Malta's role as a maritime hub.
  - Location: Birgu (Vittoriosa).
  - Practical Information: Check their website for opening hours and ticket prices.

Art Galleries: Discovering Maltese Creativity:

- Valletta Contemporary (Valletta): This contemporary art gallery showcases works by both local and international artists.
  - Highlights: Rotating exhibitions featuring contemporary painting, sculpture, photography, and video art.
  - Location: East Street, Valletta.
  - Practical Information: Check their website for current exhibitions and opening hours.
- Spazju Kreattiv (Valletta): Located at St James Cavalier, this multi-disciplinary arts center hosts exhibitions, performances, and screenings, promoting various forms of artistic expression.
  - Highlights: A diverse program of events, including visual arts exhibitions, theatre performances, film screenings, and workshops.
  - Location: Valletta.
  - Practical Information: Check their website for the program and event schedules.
- Christine X Art Gallery (Sliema): This established gallery showcases a diverse collection of contemporary art, including paintings, sculptures, and mixed media.

- o Highlights: Works by established and emerging Maltese and international artists.
- o Location: Sliema.
- o Practical Information: Check their website for current exhibitions and opening hours.

Tips for Visiting Museums and Art Galleries:

- Check Opening Hours and Ticket Prices: Museum and gallery opening hours and ticket prices can vary, so it's always a good idea to check their websites or local tourist information before your visit.
- Consider Purchasing a Malta Pass: The Malta Pass provides access to many museums and historical sites, offering good value for money if you plan to visit multiple attractions.
- Allow Sufficient Time: Some museums, like the National Museum of Archaeology and MUŻA, require several hours to fully explore their collections.
- Take Advantage of Guided Tours: Guided tours can provide valuable insights and context to the exhibits.
- Respect Museum Etiquette: Avoid touching artifacts and maintain a respectful noise level.

By exploring Malta's museums and art galleries, you can delve into the island's rich history, appreciate its artistic heritage, and gain a deeper understanding of its cultural identity.

Historical Landmarks and Heritage Sites

Malta, a tiny archipelago at the crossroads of the Mediterranean, boasts an extraordinary density of historical landmarks and heritage sites. From mysterious prehistoric temples to imposing fortifications built by the Knights of St. John, Malta's story is etched in stone, offering a captivating journey through millennia of history.

Prehistoric Wonders: Whispers of Ancient Civilizations:

- Ħaġar Qim & Mnajdra Temples: Perched dramatically on a clifftop overlooking the sea, these megalithic temples, dating back to 3600-3200 BC, are older than Stonehenge and the Egyptian pyramids.
    - History & Architecture: Ħaġar Qim features massive megaliths, some weighing several tons, while Mnajdra, nestled in a sheltered depression below, comprises three interconnected temples aligned with astronomical events. Their purpose remains debated, but they were likely centers for religious ceremonies and astronomical observations.
    - Significance: A UNESCO World Heritage Site, these temples offer invaluable insights into the lives and beliefs of Malta's prehistoric inhabitants.
    - Location: Qrendi, Southern Malta.
    - Opening Hours: Check Heritage Malta website for current hours, generally 9:00-17:00.
    - Website: Heritage Malta
    - Entry Fees: Check Heritage Malta website. Combined tickets often available.
    - Guided Tours: Audio guides and guided tours are usually available.
    - Tips: Visit early in the morning or late afternoon to avoid crowds and the midday heat.
- Ħal Saflieni Hypogeum: This unique underground burial complex, carved out of the living rock around 4000 BC, is a labyrinth of interconnected chambers, passages, and niches.
    - History & Architecture: Used as a sanctuary and necropolis for centuries, the Hypogeum features intricate decorations,

including red ochre wall paintings, and demonstrates remarkable engineering skills for its time.
- Significance: A UNESCO World Heritage Site, the Hypogeum offers a fascinating glimpse into ancient burial rituals and beliefs.
- Location: Paola, Southern Malta.
- Opening Hours: Check Heritage Malta website. Access is strictly limited, and tickets must be booked well in advance (often weeks or months).
- Website: Heritage Malta
- Entry Fees: Check Heritage Malta website.
- Guided Tours: Mandatory guided tours.
- Tips: Book tickets online as soon as possible due to limited availability.

- Tarxien Temples: This complex in Tarxien comprises four megalithic temples dating back to the Neolithic period (3600-2500 BC).
  - History & Architecture: Known for their impressive size and intricate carvings depicting animals and spirals, the Tarxien Temples provide evidence of advanced architectural and artistic skills.
  - Significance: These temples offer valuable insights into the religious practices and daily life of Malta's temple builders.
  - Location: Tarxien, Southern Malta.
  - Opening Hours: Check Heritage Malta website.
  - Website: Heritage Malta
  - Entry Fees: Check Heritage Malta website.

The Knights of St. John: Fortifications and Baroque Splendor:

- Valletta: Malta's capital, a UNESCO World Heritage City, is a living testament to the Knights of St. John's legacy.
    - History & Architecture: Built in the 16th century, Valletta's imposing fortifications, including massive bastions, high curtain walls, and ornate gates, were designed to withstand Ottoman attacks. The city's grid layout and Baroque architecture reflect the Knights' influence.
    - Significance: Valletta is a masterpiece of urban planning and a symbol of the Knights' military and cultural achievements.
    - Key Sites: St. John's Co-Cathedral, Grand Master's Palace, Upper Barrakka Gardens, City Gate.
    - Practical Information: Easily accessible by public transport. Walking is the best way to explore.
- Mdina (The Silent City): The former capital, Mdina is a fortified medieval city perched on a hilltop, offering panoramic views.
    - History & Architecture: Its narrow, winding streets, elegant palazzi, and imposing city walls evoke a sense of timelessness.
    - Significance: Mdina offers a glimpse into Malta's medieval past and its aristocratic heritage.
    - Key Sites: Mdina Cathedral, Palazzo Falson Historic House Museum, Mdina Dungeons.
    - Practical Information: Limited parking outside the city walls.
- Fort St. Elmo (Valletta): This star-shaped fort at the tip of the Sciberras Peninsula played a crucial role in the Great Siege of 1565.
    - History & Architecture: Its strategic location made it a key defensive point.

- o Significance: The fort's heroic defense during the Great Siege is a symbol of Maltese resilience. Now houses the National War Museum.
- o Practical Information: Check Heritage Malta website for opening hours and entry fees.

Tips for Visiting Historical Sites:

- Plan Ahead: Research sites and check opening hours and ticket prices.
- Heritage Malta Pass: Offers discounted entry to many sites.
- Comfortable Shoes: Essential for walking on uneven surfaces.
- Stay Hydrated: Especially during summer.
- Guided Tours: Enhance understanding and provide context.
- Respect the Sites: These are fragile historical and cultural landmarks.

Exploring Malta's historical landmarks is a journey through time, revealing the island's captivating past and enduring cultural legacy.

Religious and Spiritual Sites

Malta's deep-rooted faith is woven into the fabric of its history and landscape. The islands are dotted with magnificent churches, ancient chapels, and sacred spaces, reflecting a rich tapestry of religious traditions and cultural influences. This guide explores some of Malta's most significant religious and spiritual sites, offering insights into their history, architecture, and cultural importance.

Iconic Churches and Cathedrals:

- St. John's Co-Cathedral (Valletta): A masterpiece of Baroque architecture, St. John's Co-Cathedral is a must-see for any visitor to Malta.

- History & Architecture: Built by the Knights of St. John in the 16th century, the cathedral's austere exterior belies its opulent interior, adorned with intricate carvings, gilded decorations, and stunning paintings, including Caravaggio's masterpiece, "The Beheading of St. John the Baptist."
    - Significance: This cathedral is a symbol of the Knights' power and wealth and a testament to the Baroque artistic style.
    - Location: St. John Street, Valletta.
    - Opening Hours: Check the official website for current hours, as they vary seasonally.
    - Entry Fee: Yes.
    - Guided Tours: Audio guides are available.
    - Tips: Dress respectfully (shoulders and knees covered). Photography is allowed in some areas but without flash.
- Mosta Dome (Rotunda of St. Marija Assunta): The Mosta Dome is one of the largest unsupported domes in Europe and a prominent landmark in Malta.
    - History & Architecture: Built in the 19th century on the site of an older church, the dome's impressive size and architectural design are truly awe-inspiring. During World War II, a bomb pierced the dome during a service but miraculously failed to detonate, a story that has become a symbol of faith and resilience.
    - Significance: The dome is a testament to Maltese architectural ingenuity and a symbol of faith.
    - Location: Mosta, Central Malta.
    - Opening Hours: Check locally as times can vary.
    - Entry Fee: Usually free to enter the church (donations appreciated).

- o Tips: Take time to admire the dome's interior and learn about the "Miracle of Mosta."
- Mdina Cathedral (St. Paul's Cathedral): Located within the fortified city of Mdina, this cathedral is a significant historical and religious site.
  - o History & Architecture: The cathedral stands on the site where St. Paul is said to have converted the Roman Governor Publius to Christianity. Its Baroque architecture is impressive, with beautiful paintings and ornate decorations.
  - o Significance: This cathedral is a symbol of Malta's early Christian heritage.
  - o Location: Mdina.
  - o Opening Hours: Check locally as times can vary.
  - o Entry Fee: Yes (often includes access to the Mdina Cathedral Museum).

Lesser-Known Spiritual Retreats and Chapels:

- Sanctuary of Our Lady of Mellieħa: Overlooking Mellieħa Bay, this sanctuary is a place of pilgrimage and devotion.
  - o History & Significance: Tradition holds that St. Luke visited the site and that the Virgin Mary appeared in a nearby cave.
  - o Location: Mellieħa.
  - o Tips: The views from the sanctuary are stunning.
- Chapel of St. Agatha (Rabat): Located within the catacombs of St. Paul in Rabat, this small chapel is a significant early Christian site.
  - o History & Significance: It's believed to be one of the earliest Christian places of worship in Malta.
  - o Location: Rabat.
  - o Tips: Combine a visit with the St. Paul's Catacombs.

Local Religious Traditions and Customs:

- Village Festas: These village feasts, held throughout the summer months, are vibrant celebrations of each village's patron saint. They often include religious processions, band marches, fireworks, and street parties.
- Holy Week: Holy Week (the week leading up to Easter) is a particularly important time in Malta, with solemn processions and religious ceremonies taking place throughout the islands.
- Respectful Attire: When visiting churches and other religious sites, it's important to dress respectfully (shoulders and knees covered).

Tips for Exploring Religious Sites:

- Check Opening Hours: Opening hours can vary, especially for smaller chapels.
- Dress Respectfully: Shoulders and knees should be covered when entering religious sites.
- Maintain a Respectful Silence: Especially during services or prayer.
- Donations: Donations are often appreciated.

By exploring Malta's religious and spiritual sites, travelers can gain a deeper understanding of the island's culture, history, and the deep faith that has shaped its identity for centuries.

Local Customs and Etiquette

Malta, with its rich history and diverse cultural influences, has a unique set of customs and etiquette. Understanding and respecting these local norms will enhance your travel experience and foster positive interactions with the Maltese people.

Greetings and Introductions:

- Formal Greetings: A handshake is customary for formal introductions. When meeting someone for the first time, it's polite to use titles such as Mr., Mrs., or Ms. unless invited to use first names.
- Informal Greetings: Among friends and family, a light kiss on each cheek is a common greeting.
- Language: While English is widely spoken, learning a few basic Maltese phrases like "Bonġu" (Good morning/Good day), "Bongu" (Good evening), "Grazzi" (Thank you), and "Skużi" (Excuse me) is appreciated and shows respect for the local culture.

Dining Etiquette:

- Table Manners: Basic table manners are expected. Wait for everyone to be served before starting to eat. Keep your elbows off the table.
- Tipping: Tipping is customary in restaurants and for other services. A 10-15% tip is generally appreciated for good service.
- Eating Out: It's common for locals to enjoy leisurely meals, especially on Sundays. Don't be surprised if service is paced accordingly.

Visiting Someone's Home:

- Gifts: If invited to a Maltese home, it's customary to bring a small gift, such as a bottle of wine, flowers, or chocolates.
- Punctuality: While punctuality is appreciated, arriving slightly late (around 10-15 minutes) is generally acceptable.

- Removing Shoes: It's not always expected to remove your shoes when entering a Maltese home, but it's polite to ask if you are unsure.

Social Interactions:

- Directness: Maltese people are generally quite direct in their communication. This isn't meant to be rude but rather a sign of openness and honesty.
- Hospitality: Maltese are known for their warm hospitality. They are often willing to go out of their way to help visitors.
- Family Values: Family is highly valued in Maltese culture. It's common for extended families to live close to each other and maintain strong bonds.
- Religion: Catholicism plays a significant role in Maltese culture. Showing respect for religious traditions and customs is important.

Dress Code:

- Religious Sites: When visiting churches and other religious sites, dress respectfully. Shoulders and knees should be covered.
- General Attire: In general, casual attire is acceptable in most situations. However, dressing smartly is appreciated in more formal settings, such as fine dining restaurants.

Other Important Considerations:

- Public Displays of Affection: While holding hands is generally acceptable, excessive public displays of affection are less common.
- Photography: It's generally acceptable to take photos in public places, but it's polite to ask for permission before photographing people, especially in villages or during religious processions.

- Noise Levels: Be mindful of noise levels, especially in residential areas and during siesta time (usually in the early afternoon).

Tips for Respectful Interaction:

- Be Polite and Courteous: Simple gestures like saying "please" and "thank you" go a long way.
- Show Interest in Maltese Culture: Asking questions about local customs and traditions demonstrates respect and a genuine interest in learning more.
- Respect Religious Traditions: Dress respectfully when visiting religious sites and be mindful of local customs during religious events.
- Be Patient and Understanding: Remember that cultural differences exist. Be patient and understanding of any unfamiliar customs or behaviors.
- Smile and Be Friendly: A smile and a friendly demeanor can help bridge cultural gaps and create positive interactions.

By being mindful of these local customs and cultural etiquette, you can ensure respectful and rewarding interactions with the Maltese people, enriching your overall travel experience.

CHAPTER TEN

PRACTICAL INFORMATION

Tourist Information Centers

Malta's Tourist Information Centers (TICs) are invaluable resources for visitors, offering a wealth of information and assistance to help you make the most of your trip. These centers provide essential services, from maps and brochures to multilingual support and local insights.

Key Tourist Information Centers:

While Malta Tourism Authority (MTA) is the main tourism body, physical information centers are less common than in some destinations. Information is readily available online and through other means, but here's how to find assistance:

- Malta International Airport (MLA): Upon arrival, you'll find information desks within the arrivals hall. These desks can provide basic information, maps, and brochures to get you started.
- Online Resources: The Malta Tourism Authority website (www.visitmalta.com) is the most comprehensive source of information. It offers detailed information on attractions, accommodations, dining, events, transportation, and more. It's highly recommended to consult this website before and during your trip.
- Local Councils and Municipalities: Local councils and municipalities often have their own information points or websites with details specific to their area. These can be

helpful for finding information about local events, attractions, and services.
- Hotel Concierges: Hotel concierges can also provide valuable information and assistance to guests, including recommendations for attractions, restaurants, and tours.

Services Offered:

While physical centers may be limited, the available resources provide the following:

- Maps and Brochures: Maps of Malta and Gozo, as well as brochures and leaflets on various attractions, activities, and events.
- Multilingual Assistance: Staff at the airport information desks and within hotels generally speak English and often other languages. The MTA website is also available in multiple languages.
- Local Insights and Recommendations: Information on local events, festivals, and cultural activities. Recommendations for attractions, accommodations, restaurants, and tours.
- Transportation Information: Information on public transport, including bus routes and schedules, as well as information on taxis and car rentals.
- Assistance with Bookings: Some centers or hotel concierges may be able to assist with booking tours, excursions, and accommodations.

Utilizing Tourist Information Resources:

- Plan Ahead: Consult the MTA website (www.visitmalta.com) before your trip to research attractions, plan your itinerary, and find information on transportation and accommodations.

- Grab a Map: Upon arrival at the airport, pick up a map of Malta and Gozo.
- Ask for Recommendations: Don't hesitate to ask hotel staff or locals for recommendations on restaurants, attractions, and hidden gems.
- Check Local Listings: Look for local newspapers, magazines, and online listings for information on events and activities.
- Use Online Resources: The MTA website and other online resources are invaluable tools for planning your trip and finding information during your stay.

Practical Tips:

- Download Offline Maps: Consider downloading offline maps on your smartphone for easy navigation, especially if you won't have consistent internet access.
- Use Public Wi-Fi: Many cafes, restaurants, and hotels offer free Wi-Fi, which you can use to access online resources and information.
- Contact the MTA Online: If you have specific questions or need assistance before your trip, you can contact the MTA through their website.

While traditional physical tourist information centers are less common, Malta provides ample resources through its robust online presence, airport information desks, and helpful locals. By utilizing these resources, you can ensure you have access to the information and support you need to enhance your Maltese adventure.

Local Guides and Tour Operators

Exploring Malta with a local guide or through a reputable tour operator can significantly enhance your travel experience, providing deeper insights into the islands' history, culture, and hidden gems.

This section highlights some options for enriching your visit with expert local knowledge.

Types of Tours Available:

- Historical Tours: These tours focus on Malta's rich history, covering prehistoric temples, medieval cities, and sites related to the Knights of St. John and World War II. Guides often have specialized knowledge in archaeology, history, or art history.
- Cultural Experiences: These tours immerse you in Maltese culture, including visits to local markets, traditional villages, craft workshops, and participation in local festivals or events.
- Adventure Excursions: These tours cater to more active travelers, offering activities like hiking, rock climbing, kayaking, diving, and boat trips around the islands.
- Boat Tours and Cruises: Explore Malta's stunning coastline, visit secluded coves, and discover the neighboring islands of Gozo and Comino by boat. Options range from short harbor cruises to full-day excursions.
- Food Tours: Discover Maltese cuisine with guided food tours that explore local markets, traditional restaurants, and sample local delicacies.
- Customized Itineraries: Some tour operators offer customized itineraries tailored to your specific interests and preferences. This is a great option for those who want a more personalized experience.

Choosing the Right Tour Operator:

- Reputation and Reviews: Look for tour operators with positive online reviews and testimonials. Check travel websites and forums for recommendations.

- Licensing and Accreditation: Ensure the tour operator is licensed and accredited by the Malta Tourism Authority (MTA).
- Guide Qualifications: Inquire about the qualifications and experience of the guides. Look for guides with specialized knowledge in your areas of interest.
- Group Size: Consider the group size of the tour. Smaller groups often offer a more personalized experience.
- Language Options: Ensure the tour is offered in your preferred language.
- Inclusions and Exclusions: Carefully review the tour itinerary and inclusions, such as transportation, entrance fees, and meals.

What to Expect from Guided Tours:

- Expert Knowledge: Guides provide valuable insights and information that you might not find in guidebooks.
- Convenience: Tours often include transportation and entrance fees, making it easier to visit multiple attractions.
- Local Perspectives: Guides offer local perspectives and insights into Maltese culture and traditions.
- Personalized Experience: Smaller group tours or private tours offer a more personalized experience.

Finding Local Guides and Tour Operators:

- Online Search: Search online for "Malta tours," "Malta guided tours," or "Malta tour operators."
- Tourist Information Websites: The MTA website (www.visitmalta.com) may list licensed tour operators.
- Hotel Concierges: Hotel concierges can often recommend reputable tour operators and help with bookings.

- Local Tourist Offices: Local tourist offices in towns and villages may also have information on local guides and tours.

Practical Information:

- Contact Details: Contact details for tour operators can usually be found on their websites or brochures.
- Tour Schedules: Tour schedules vary depending on the tour and the time of year.
- Pricing: Pricing varies depending on the tour length, inclusions, and group size.
- Booking Tips: Booking in advance is recommended, especially for popular tours and during peak season.

By choosing a reputable local guide or tour operator, you can unlock the hidden gems of Malta and create a more enriching and memorable travel experience.

Essential Useful Phrases

While English is widely spoken in Malta, learning a few basic Maltese phrases can greatly enhance your travel experience and foster connections with locals. This mini-phrasebook provides essential expressions for common travel situations.

Basic Greetings:

- Hello: Bonġu (Bon-ju) – Used throughout the day.
- Good evening: Bongu (Bon-ju) – Used after sunset.
- Goodbye: Saħħa (Sah-ha)
- Please: Jekk jogħġbok (Yek yok-bok)
- Thank you: Grazzi (Grat-tsi)
- You're welcome: M'hemmx għalfejn (Mhemmsh ghal-feyn) or Prosit (Pro-sit)
- Excuse me: Skużi (Skuh-tsi)

- Yes: Iva (Ee-va)
- No: Le (Leh)

Asking for Directions:

- Where is…? Fejn hi…? (Feyn hee…?)
- How do I get to…? Kif nasal sa…? (Keef na-sal sa…?)
- The bus stop: L-istazzjon tal-karozza tal-linja (L-istat-tsjun tal-ka-rot-tsa tal-lin-ya)
- The airport: L-ajruport (L-ay-ru-port)
- The city center: Iċ-ċentru tal-belt (Ich-chen-tru tal-belt)
- Left: Xellug (Shel-lug)
- Right: Lemin (Le-min)
- Straight ahead: Dritt (Drit)

Ordering Food:

- A table for one/two, please: Mejda għal wieħed/tnejn, jekk jogħġbok (May-da ghal wee-hed/tneyn, yek yok-bok)
- The menu, please: Il-menu, jekk jogħġbok (Il-me-nu, yek yok-bok)
- I would like…: Nixtieq… (Nish-tee-ek…)
- Water: Ilma (Il-ma)
- Beer: Birra (Bir-ra)
- Wine: Inbid (In-bid)
- The bill, please: Il-kont, jekk jogħġbok (Il-kont, yek yok-bok)

Making Purchases:

- How much does this cost? Kemm jiswa dan? (Kemm yis-wa dan?)
- I would like to buy this: Nixtieq nixtri dan (Nish-tee-ek nish-tree dan)
- Open: Miftuħ (Mif-tuh)

- Closed: Magħluq (Magh-luq)

Seeking Assistance:

- Do you speak English? Titkellem bl-Ingliż? (Tit-kel-lem bling-leez?)
- I need help: Għandi bżonn l-għajnuna (Ghan-di bzonn l-ghay-nu-na)
- Police: Pulizija (Pu-li-tsi-ya)
- Hospital: Sptar (Sp-tar)

Additional Tips:

- Pronunciation: Maltese pronunciation can be challenging for English speakers. Focus on the stressed syllables and listen carefully to native speakers. Online resources and language learning apps can be helpful.
- Politeness: Even a few basic phrases spoken with a smile and polite demeanor will be greatly appreciated by locals.
- Don't Be Afraid to Try: Don't be afraid to try speaking Maltese, even if you make mistakes. Locals are usually very encouraging and appreciative of the effort.

While this list provides a starting point, remember that language learning is an ongoing process. Using these phrases will not only help you navigate daily situations but also connect you with Maltese culture in a more meaningful way.

Travel Insurance

Travel insurance is a vital component of any trip, providing a safety net against unforeseen events and unexpected expenses. While Malta is generally a safe destination, travel insurance offers peace of mind and financial protection should anything go wrong. This section emphasizes the importance of obtaining comprehensive travel insurance coverage for a worry-free journey.

Why Travel Insurance is Essential for Malta:

Even with careful planning, unexpected events can disrupt your travel plans. Travel insurance protects you from financial losses and provides assistance in various situations, including:

- Medical Emergencies: Medical expenses abroad can be substantial. Travel insurance covers medical treatment, hospitalization, emergency evacuation, and repatriation in case of illness or injury.
- Trip Cancellations or Interruptions: If you need to cancel or interrupt your trip due to unforeseen circumstances such as illness, family emergencies, or natural disasters, travel insurance can reimburse your non-refundable travel costs.
- Lost or Stolen Belongings: Travel insurance can cover the cost of replacing lost or stolen luggage, personal belongings, and travel documents.
- Flight Delays or Missed Connections: If your flight is delayed or you miss a connection due to unforeseen circumstances, travel insurance can cover expenses such as meals, accommodation, and transportation.
- Personal Liability: In some cases, travel insurance can provide coverage for legal expenses if you are held responsible for causing damage or injury to others.

Types of Travel Insurance Policies:

- Single Trip Insurance: This type of policy covers a single trip with specific start and end dates. It's suitable for most leisure travelers.

- Multi-Trip Insurance (Annual Travel Insurance): This policy provides coverage for multiple trips within a year. It's ideal for frequent travelers.
- Comprehensive Travel Insurance: This offers the broadest coverage, including medical emergencies, trip cancellations, lost baggage, and personal liability.

Optional Add-ons and Upgrades:

You can often customize your travel insurance policy with optional add-ons or upgrades to suit your specific needs:

- Adventure Activities Coverage: If you plan to participate in adventure activities like diving, rock climbing, or water sports, ensure your policy covers these activities.
- Pre-existing Medical Conditions Coverage: If you have any pre-existing medical conditions, declare them to your insurer to ensure you are adequately covered.
- Cruise Coverage: If your trip includes a cruise, consider adding cruise-specific coverage, which may include missed port departures, cabin confinement, and medical emergencies at sea.

Choosing a Reputable Travel Insurance Provider:

- Research and Compare: Compare policies from different providers to find the best coverage and price.
- Check Reviews and Ratings: Look for reviews and ratings from other travelers to assess the provider's reputation.
- Read the Policy Carefully: Understand the terms and conditions of the policy, including what is and isn't covered.
- Check the Coverage Limits: Ensure the coverage limits are sufficient for your needs.

Tips for Understanding Your Policy:

- Understand the Exclusions: Be aware of any exclusions in the policy, such as certain pre-existing medical conditions or activities.
- Keep Your Policy Documents Handy: Carry a copy of your policy documents with you and store a digital copy securely online.
- Know the Claims Process: Familiarize yourself with the claims process in case you need to make a claim.

Travel insurance is a small investment that can provide significant financial protection and peace of mind during your travels. By obtaining adequate coverage, you can focus on enjoying your Maltese adventure knowing you are protected from unexpected events and emergencies.

Emergency Numbers and Important Contacts

Knowing who to contact in case of an emergency is crucial when traveling. This section provides a list of essential emergency numbers and important contacts for your stay in Malta.

Emergency Numbers:

- Emergency (Police, Ambulance, Fire Brigade): 112 (This is the Europe-wide emergency number and will connect you to the appropriate service.)
- Police (Non-Emergency): 2122 4001-9
- Ambulance (Non-Emergency): 2124 1251
- Fire Brigade (Non-Emergency): 2124 4371
- Mater Dei Hospital (Main Public Hospital): 2545 0000

Other Important Contacts:

- Malta Tourism Authority (MTA): 2291 5000 (For tourist information and assistance)
- Visitor Helpline (Malta Tourism Authority): +356 2169 2447
- Local Police Stations: Each locality has its own police station. You can find contact details on the Malta Police Force website.
- Your Country's Embassy or Consulate: It's important to know the contact details of your country's embassy or consulate in Malta in case of emergencies involving your citizenship or travel documents. You can find this information on your government's website.

Important Information to Keep Handy:

- Copies of Important Documents: Make copies of your passport, visa, travel insurance policy, and other important documents. Store these separately from the originals and keep digital copies securely online.
- Travel Insurance Details: Keep your travel insurance policy number and emergency contact information readily available.
- Emergency Contact Information: Have a list of emergency contacts at home and in Malta, including phone numbers and email addresses.
- Accommodation Details: Keep a record of your accommodation address and phone number.

Tips for Staying Safe:

- Be Aware of Your Surroundings: Be mindful of your belongings and surroundings, especially in crowded areas.
- Keep Valuables Secure: Store valuables in a safe place, such as a hotel safe or a secure bag.

- Use Reputable Transportation: Use licensed taxis or reputable ride-hailing services.
- Stay Hydrated: Especially during the summer months, drink plenty of water to avoid dehydration.
- Be Sun Smart: Use sunscreen, wear a hat, and seek shade during the hottest part of the day.
- Inform Someone of Your Itinerary: Let someone know your travel plans and itinerary, especially if you are traveling alone.

In Case of Emergency:

- Stay Calm: In an emergency, try to stay calm and assess the situation.
- Call the Appropriate Emergency Number: If you need immediate assistance, call 112.
- Provide Clear Information: When contacting emergency services, provide clear and concise information about your location and the nature of the emergency.
- Contact Your Travel Insurance Provider: If you need medical assistance or have experienced a loss covered by your travel insurance, contact your insurance provider as soon as possible.
- Contact Your Embassy or Consulate: If you need assistance with your travel documents or have other consular issues, contact your country's embassy or consulate.

By being prepared and having access to these emergency numbers and important contacts, you can ensure a safer and more secure trip to Malta.

Sustainable Travel Practices

Malta's stunning natural beauty and rich cultural heritage are precious resources that deserve our protection. As travelers, we have a responsibility to minimize our environmental impact and contribute to sustainable tourism practices. This section provides tips on how to travel responsibly in Malta, ensuring that future generations can enjoy the islands' unique charm.

Reducing Waste:

- Reusable Water Bottles: Bring a reusable water bottle and refill it at your accommodation or at public water fountains. This helps reduce plastic waste from disposable water bottles.
- Reusable Shopping Bags: Carry reusable shopping bags for groceries and souvenirs, avoiding the need for plastic bags.
- Say No to Single-Use Plastics: Avoid using single-use plastics such as straws, cutlery, and disposable containers.

Conserving Energy and Water:

- Choose Eco-Friendly Accommodations: Look for accommodations that have implemented sustainable practices, such as energy-efficient lighting, water-saving fixtures, and recycling programs.
- Conserve Water: Take shorter showers, reuse towels, and report any leaks to your accommodation.
- Conserve Energy: Turn off lights, air conditioning, and other appliances when not in use.

Supporting Local Businesses and Artisans:

- Shop Locally: Support local businesses and artisans by purchasing locally made products and souvenirs. This helps support the local economy and preserves traditional crafts.
- Eat at Local Restaurants: Choose local restaurants and try traditional Maltese cuisine. This supports local farmers and food producers.

- Visit Local Markets: Visit local markets to experience the local culture and purchase fresh, seasonal produce.

Choosing Eco-Friendly Transportation:

- Public Transport: Utilize Malta's extensive public bus network, which is an affordable and environmentally friendly way to get around the islands.
- Walking and Cycling: Explore towns and villages on foot or by bicycle. This is a great way to experience the local atmosphere and reduce your carbon footprint.
- Ferry Travel: Use ferries to travel between Malta and Gozo, which is a more environmentally friendly option than flying.

Respecting Wildlife and Natural Habitats:

- Observe Wildlife Responsibly: Observe wildlife from a safe distance and avoid disturbing their natural habitat.
- Avoid Touching or Feeding Wild Animals: Do not touch or feed wild animals, as this can disrupt their natural behavior.
- Protect Marine Environments: When swimming or snorkeling, avoid touching or disturbing coral reefs and other marine life.

Sustainable Tourism Initiatives and Volunteering:

- Check for Eco-Certified Tour Operators: Choose tour operators that are certified for their sustainable practices.
- Volunteer Opportunities: Look for opportunities to volunteer with local conservation organizations or participate in community-based projects.

By adopting these sustainable travel practices, you can contribute to preserving Malta's natural beauty and cultural heritage for future generations. Remember that even small changes in your travel habits can make a big difference.

Useful Apps and Websites

To make your travel experience to Malta smoother and more enjoyable, there are several apps and websites that can help you with everything from navigation and transportation to restaurant reservations and activity bookings. Here's a selection of essential tools to consider during your visit:

Transportation and Navigation Apps

- Tallinja
    - Website: www.tallinja.com
    - App: Tallinja Bus (Available on iOS and Android)
    - This is the official app for public transport in Malta, offering bus routes, schedules, and real-time updates. You can check the nearest bus stops, plan your journey, and even purchase travel cards or single tickets.
- Bolt
    - App: Bolt (Available on iOS and Android)
    - For those preferring a more direct form of transportation, Bolt (formerly Taxify) is a popular ridesharing app in Malta. It provides a convenient and often cheaper alternative to taxis.
- Google Maps
    - App: Google Maps (Available on iOS and Android)
    - A must-have for navigation, Google Maps provides accurate directions for both walking and driving, alongside public transport options. It also gives you real-time traffic updates, making it easy to get around the island.

Dining and Restaurant Reservations

- TheFork
  - App: TheFork (Available on iOS and Android)
  - This app allows you to search for restaurants, read reviews, check menus, and make reservations. It also often offers special discounts for bookings made through the app.
- Tripadvisor
  - Website & App: www.tripadvisor.com
  - Tripadvisor is great for reading reviews of restaurants, cafes, and bars in Malta. You can search based on your preferences, such as budget, location, or type of cuisine, and book reservations directly.
- EatWith
  - Website & App: www.eatwith.com
  - For a unique local experience, EatWith connects travelers with locals who host home dinners or cooking classes. It's perfect for those looking to enjoy authentic Maltese meals in an intimate setting.

Activity Booking

- Viator
  - Website & App: www.viator.com
  - Viator offers a wide range of tours, activities, and experiences across Malta. From boat trips to historical tours, the app lets you book popular activities directly from your phone.
- GetYourGuide
  - Website & App: www.getyourguide.com

- Another excellent app for booking guided tours, skip-the-line tickets, and unique experiences, GetYourGuide offers a comprehensive selection of Malta's attractions.

Currency and Budgeting

- XE Currency
    - App: XE Currency (Available on iOS and Android)
    - If you're traveling from outside the EU, XE Currency will help you track the exchange rates in real-time. It's perfect for budgeting and understanding the value of your money in Euros.
- Revolut
    - App: Revolut (Available on iOS and Android)
    - A great app for managing finances while traveling, Revolut allows you to exchange currency at competitive rates, make payments, and track spending all in one place.

Local Information

- Malta Tourism Authority
    - Website: www.visitmalta.com
    - This is the official tourism website for Malta. It provides a wealth of information on things to do, festivals, events, and practical travel tips. You'll also find detailed itineraries and guides for different types of travelers.
- Malta Weather
    - Website: www.maltaweather.com
    - Keep track of the weather conditions during your trip with this reliable source. It offers up-to-date weather forecasts, including hourly predictions, so you can plan your outdoor activities accordingly.

Language and Translation

- Google Translate
    - App: Google Translate (Available on iOS and Android)
    - While Maltese and English are both official languages, some local expressions or signs may be in Maltese. Google Translate can be used to quickly translate text, signs, and even conversations in real time.
- Duolingo
    - App: Duolingo (Available on iOS and Android)
    - If you want to learn a few words of Maltese before your trip, Duolingo is a fun and easy way to get started with basic phrases and vocabulary.

Health and Safety

- Malta Health Services
    - Website: www.health.gov.mt
    - For travelers needing information about healthcare services, insurance, or emergency contact details, the official Malta Health Services website is the place to go.
- TravelSafe
    - App: TravelSafe (Available on iOS and Android)
    - TravelSafe offers helpful information on the emergency numbers for different countries, including Malta, along with medical facilities and advice on how to deal with health emergencies while traveling.

By utilizing these apps and websites, you'll be able to navigate Malta with ease, enhance your travel experience, and ensure your trip is well-planned and stress-free.

CONCLUSION

Reflecting On Your Maltese Adventure

As we reach the end of this guide, we hope you've gained a comprehensive understanding of the captivating archipelago that is Malta. From its prehistoric temples, older than Stonehenge, to the magnificent fortifications built by the Knights of St. John, Malta offers a journey through time, a living testament to millennia of history and cultural exchange.

We've explored the bustling streets of Valletta, a UNESCO World Heritage city, a masterpiece of Baroque architecture, and the serene, fortified city of Mdina, offering a glimpse into Malta's medieval past. We've ventured to Gozo, Malta's sister island, with its tranquil landscapes, stunning coastlines, and the legendary Azure Window (now a breathtaking diving site). We've also delved into the vibrant local culture, from the colorful village feasts to the delicious Mediterranean cuisine, influenced by centuries of diverse civilizations.

This guide has aimed to equip you with the knowledge and inspiration to explore Malta to its fullest. Whether you're drawn to the island's rich history, its stunning natural beauty, its vibrant culture, or its tranquil atmosphere, Malta offers a unique and unforgettable experience.

We encourage you to embrace the spirit of adventure and exploration. Wander through ancient streets, discover hidden coves, immerse yourself in local traditions, and savor the flavors of Maltese cuisine. Take the time to connect with the friendly locals, who are known for their warm hospitality and welcoming nature.

Malta is more than just a destination; it's an experience that will stay with you long after you've left its shores. It's a place where history comes alive, where natural beauty captivates the senses, and where the warmth of the Mediterranean spirit embraces you.

We hope this guide has been a valuable resource in planning your Maltese adventure. We've strived to provide accurate and up-to-date information to help you navigate the islands with confidence and create lasting memories.

Thank you for choosing this travel guide as your companion. We wish you safe travels, unforgettable experiences, and a journey filled with discovery and wonder, not just in Malta, but in all your future adventures. May your travels be filled with joy, enriching encounters, and a deep appreciation for the diverse beauty of our world. Saħħa (Goodbye)!

Printed in Dunstable, United Kingdom